**U.S. Department
of Transportation**

Federal Aviation
Administration

Advisory

Circular

MW00955798

Subject: Small Unmanned Aircraft System (Small UAS)	**Date:** 2/1/21	**AC No:** 107-2A
	Initiated by: AFS-800	**Change:**

This advisory circular (AC) provides guidance for conducting small unmanned aircraft systems (UAS) operations in the National Airspace System (NAS) in accordance with Title 14 of the Code of Federal Regulations (14 CFR) part 107.

Robert C. Carty
Deputy Executive Director, Flight Standards Service

CONTENTS

Paragraph   **Page**

List of Figures

List of Tables

CHAPTER 1. GENERAL

1.1 **Purpose of This Advisory Circular (AC).** This AC provides guidance in the areas of airman (remote pilot) certification, aircraft registration and marking, aircraft airworthiness, and the operation of small Unmanned Aircraft Systems (UAS) in the National Airspace System (NAS) to promote compliance with the requirements of Title 14 of the Code of Federal Regulations (14 CFR) part 107.

1.1.1 <u>Effects of Guidance</u>. The contents of this document do not have the force and effect of law and are not meant to bind the public in any way. This document is intended only to provide clarity to the public regarding existing requirements under the law or agency policies. It does not provide, nor is it intended to provide, a legal interpretation of the regulations. This AC uses mandatory terms, such as "must," when the language is describing an established statutory or regulatory requirement. This AC does not change, add to, or delete regulatory requirements or authorize deviations from regulatory requirements or restrictions.

1.1.2 <u>Part 107 Provisions</u>. This AC is not intended to cover every provision of part 107. Rather, this AC is intended to provide guidance on those provisions of part 107 where additional information may be helpful. The Federal Aviation Administration (FAA) emphasizes, however, that persons subject to part 107 are responsible for complying with every applicable provision of part 107, regardless of whether the provision is discussed in this AC.

1.1.3 <u>Privacy-Related Laws</u>. Part 107 operators should be aware that State and local authorities may enact privacy-related laws specific to UAS operations. The FAA encourages small UAS operators to review those laws prior to operating their UAS. The National Telecommunications and Information Administration (NTIA) has also published the Voluntary Best Practices for UAS Privacy, Transparency, and Accountability (dated May 18, 2016), available at https://www.ntia.doc.gov/files/ntia/publications/uas_privacy_best_practices_6-21-16.pdf. This document outlines and describes voluntary best practices that small UAS operators could take to advance UAS privacy, transparency, and accountability for the private and commercial use of UAS.

1.2 **Where You Can Find This AC.** You can find this AC on the FAA's website at https://www.faa.gov/regulations_policies/advisory_circulars.

1.3 **What This AC Cancels.** AC 107-2, Small Unmanned Aircraft Systems (sUAS), dated June 21, 2016, is canceled.

1.4 **Request for Information.** Direct comments and suggestions for improving this publication to:

Federal Aviation Administration
General Aviation and Commercial Division (AFS-800)
55 M Street SE, 8th Floor, Zone 1
Washington, DC 20003

1.5 **AC Feedback Form.** For your convenience, the AC Feedback Form is the last page of this AC. Note any deficiencies found, clarifications needed, or suggested improvements regarding the contents of this AC on the Feedback Form.

CHAPTER 2. REFERENCES

2.1 Related Code of Federal Regulations (CFR) Parts. The following regulations and parts can be found at https://www.faa.gov/regulations_policies/faa_regulations/.

2.1.1 Title 14 CFR.

- Part 1, Definitions and Abbreviations.

- Part 43, Maintenance, Preventive Maintenance, Rebuilding, and Alteration.

- Part 47, Aircraft Registration.

- Part 48, Registration and Marking Requirements for Small Unmanned Aircraft.

- Part 71, Designation of Class A, B, C, D, and E Airspace Areas; Air Traffic Service Routes; and Reporting Points.

- Part 73, Special Use Airspace.

- Part 89, Remote Identification of Unmanned Aircraft.

- Part 91, General Operating and Flight Rules.

- Part 93, Special Air Traffic Rules.

- Part 99, Security Control of Air Traffic.

- Part 107, Small Unmanned Aircraft Systems.

2.1.2 Title 47 CFR. Part 87, Aviation Services.

2.1.3 Title 49 CFR. Part 830, Notification and Reporting of Aircraft Accidents or Incidents and Overdue Aircraft, and Preservation of Aircraft Wreckage, Mail, Cargo, and Records.

2.2 Notices to Air Missions (NOTAM). Information on how to obtain NOTAMs can be found at https://pilotweb.nas.faa.gov/PilotWeb/.

2.2.1 Additional resources to create NOTAMs, check weather, and prepare flight plans can be found at https://www.1800wxbrief.com/.

2.3 Related Reading Material. The following listed reference materials contain additional information necessary to ensure safe operations in the NAS. A small UAS operator may want to consider seeking out additional publications to supplement the lists below.

2.3.1 FAA ACs and Directives (current editions). You can find the current editions of the following publications on the FAA websites https://www.faa.gov/regulations_policies/advisory_circulars/ and https://www.faa.gov/regulations_policies/orders_notices/.

- AC 00-6, Aviation Weather.

- AC 00-45, Aviation Weather Services.

- AC 60-28, FAA English Language Standard for an FAA Certificate Issued Under 14 CFR Parts 61, 63, 65, and 107.

- AC 61-141, Flight Instructors as Certifying Officials for Student Pilot and Remote Pilot Applicants.

- AC 120-92, Safety Management Systems for Aviation Service Providers.

- FAA Order JO 7110.10, Air Traffic Organization Policy, Flight Services.

- FAA Order JO 7110.65, Air Traffic Organization Policy, Air Traffic Control.

- FAA Order JO 7200.23, Air Traffic Organization Policy, Processing of Unmanned Aircraft Systems Requests.

- FAA Order JO 7210.3, Air Traffic Organization Policy, Facility Operation and Administration.

- FAA Order JO 7400.11, Air Traffic Organization Policy, Airspace Designations and Reporting Points.

- FAA Order 8130.34, Airworthiness Certification of Unmanned Aircraft Systems and Optionally Piloted Aircraft.

- FAA Order 8900.1, Volume 16, Unmanned Aircraft Systems.

2.3.2 <u>Additional FAA Online/Mobile Sources.</u>

- UAS website: https://www.faa.gov/uas/.

- UAS Registration website: https://faadronezone.faa.gov/.

- B4UFLY mobile app.

- UAS Flight Planning, NOTAMs, temporary flight restrictions (TFR): https://www.1800wxbrief.com/ and https://tfr.faa.gov.

- FAA Safety website: https://www.faasafety.gov.

- FAA UAS Data Delivery System website: https://udds-faa.opendata.arcgis.com/.

- FAA Waiver Safety Explanation Guidelines for Part 107 Waiver Applications: https://www.faa.gov/uas/commercial_operators/part_107_waivers/waiver_safety_exp lanation_guidelines/.

- FAA Integrated Airman Certification and Rating Application (IACRA): https://iacra.faa.gov/iacra.

- Airman Certificate Testing Service (ACTS): https://www.faa.gov/training_testing/testing/ACTS/.

- Flight Standards District Offices (FSDO): https://www.faa.gov/about/office_org/field_offices/fsdo.

2.3.3   <u>FAA Handbooks, Manuals, and Other Publications</u>. You can find the following handbooks, manuals, and other publications on the FAA website at https://www.faa.gov/regulations_policies/handbooks_manuals/.

- Aeronautical Information Manual (AIM): https://www.faa.gov/air_traffic/publications/.

- Aeronautical Charts (Digital): https://www.faa.gov/air_traffic/flight_info/aeronav/digital_products/.

- Pilot/Controller Glossary: https://www.faa.gov/air_traffic/publications/.

- Pilot's Handbook of Aeronautical Knowledge: https://www.faa.gov/regulations_policies/handbooks_manuals/aviation/phak/.

- Risk Management Handbook: https://www.faa.gov/sites/faa.gov/files/regulations_policies/handbooks_manuals/aviation/risk_management_hb_change_1.pdf.

- Remote Pilot – Small Unmanned Aircraft Systems Airman Certification Standards (ACS): https://www.faa.gov/training_testing/testing/acs/media/uas_acs.pdf.

- Unmanned Aircraft Systems Operating Handbook: https://www.faa.gov/about/office_org/headquarters_offices/avs/offices/afx/afs/afs600/afs630/.

2.3.4   <u>Statutory Resources</u>.

- Public Law (PL) <u>112-95</u> (Feb. 14, 2012), Title III, Subtitle B—Unmanned Aircraft Systems.

- PL <u>114-190</u> (July 15, 2016), Title II, Subtitle B—UAS Safety.

- PL <u>115-254</u> (Oct. 5, 2018), Title III, Subtitle B—Unmanned Aircraft Systems.

CHAPTER 3. BACKGROUND

3.1 PL 112-95, Title III, Subtitle B. In 2012, Congress passed the FAA Modernization and Reform Act of 2012, PL 112-95. Section 333 of PL 112-95 directed the Secretary of Transportation to determine whether UAS operations posing the least amount of public risk and no threat to national security could safely be operated in the NAS and, if so, to establish requirements for the safe operation of these systems in the NAS. As part of its ongoing efforts to integrate UAS operations in the NAS and in accordance with Section 333, in June 2016, the FAA issued a final rule adding part 107, integrating civil small UAS into the NAS. Part 107 allows small UAS operations for many different purposes without requiring airworthiness certification, exemption, or a Certificate of Waiver or Authorization (COA).

3.2 Organization of Part 107. The FAA addresses aviation safety in three key areas: personnel, equipment, and operations. The FAA assesses each of these areas both independently to meet current regulations and standards, as well as collectively to ensure no conflicts exist overall that would create an unsafe condition. This approach allows the FAA to be flexible in responding to the needs of the aviation community while still being able to establish standards for future growth and development. To that end, part 107 contains subparts that focus on each of these key aviation safety areas specific to small UAS, and the chapters in this AC are organized in the same manner.

CHAPTER 4. PART 107 SUBPART A, GENERAL

4.1 **Applicability.** This chapter provides guidance regarding the applicability of part 107 to civil small unmanned aircraft operations conducted within the NAS. However, part 107 does not apply to the following:

1. Limited recreational operations of UAS that occur in accordance with Title 49 of the United States Code (49 U.S.C.) § 44809[1];

2. Operations conducted outside the United States;

3. Amateur rockets;

4. Moored balloons;

5. Unmanned free balloons;

6. Kites;

7. Public aircraft operations; and

8. Air carrier operations.

4.2 **Definitions.** The following defined terms are used throughout this AC:

4.2.1 Applicant. A person who submits a declaration of compliance (DOC) to the FAA for review and acceptance. An applicant may be anyone who designs, produces, or modifies a small unmanned aircraft.

4.2.2 Control Station (CS). An interface used by the remote pilot or the person manipulating the controls to control the flightpath of the small unmanned aircraft.

4.2.3 Corrective Lenses. Spectacles or contact lenses.

4.2.4 Declaration of Compliance (DOC). A record submitted to the FAA that certifies the small unmanned aircraft conforms to the Category 2 or Category 3 requirements under part 107 subpart D, as described in Chapter 8, Small Unmanned Aircraft Over People.

---

[1] Title 49 U.S.C. § 44809(a) states that a person may operate a small unmanned aircraft without specific certification or operating authority from the FAA if the operation adheres to all of the following limitations: (1) the aircraft is flown strictly for recreational purposes; (2) the aircraft is operated in accordance with or within the programming of a community-based organization's set of safety guidelines that are developed in coordination with the FAA; (3) the aircraft is flown within Visual Line of Sight (VLOS) of the person operating the aircraft or a visual observer (VO) co-located and in direct communication with the operator; (4) the aircraft is operated in a manner that does not interfere with and gives way to any manned aircraft; (5) in Class B, Class C, or Class D airspace or within the lateral boundaries of the surface area of Class E airspace designated for an airport, the operator obtains prior authorization from the Administrator or designee before operating and complies with all airspace restrictions and prohibitions; (6) in Class G airspace, the aircraft is flown from the surface to not more than 400 feet above ground level (AGL) and complies with all airspace restrictions and prohibitions; (7) the operator has passed an aeronautical knowledge and safety test described in § 44809(g) and maintains proof of test passage to be made available to the Administrator or law enforcement upon request; and (8) the aircraft is registered and marked in accordance with 49 U.S.C. chapter 441 and proof of registration is made available to the Administrator or a designee of the Administrator or law enforcement upon request.

4.2.5 <u>Means of Compliance (MOC)</u>. The method an applicant uses to show its small UAS would not exceed the applicable injury severity limit upon impact with a human being, does not contain any exposed rotating parts that would cause lacerations, and does not have any safety defects.

4.2.6 <u>Person Manipulating the Controls</u>. A person other than the remote pilot in command (PIC) who is controlling the flight of a small unmanned aircraft under the supervision of the remote PIC.

4.2.7 <u>Remote Pilot in Command (Remote PIC or Remote Pilot)</u>. A person who holds a Remote Pilot Certificate with a small UAS rating and has the final authority and responsibility for the operation and safety of a small unmanned aircraft operation conducted under part 107.

4.2.8 <u>Small Unmanned Aircraft</u>. A small unmanned aircraft weighing less than 55 pounds, including everything that is on board or otherwise attached to the aircraft, and can be flown without the possibility of direct human intervention from within or on the aircraft.

4.2.9 <u>Small Unmanned Aircraft System (small UAS)</u>. A small unmanned aircraft and its associated elements (including communication links and the components that control the small unmanned aircraft) that are required for the safe and efficient operation of the small unmanned aircraft in the NAS.

4.2.10 <u>Unmanned Aircraft</u>. An aircraft operated without the possibility of direct human intervention from within or on the aircraft (part 1, § 1.1).

4.2.11 <u>Visual Observer (VO)</u>. A person the remote PIC designates as a crewmember who assists the small unmanned aircraft remote PIC and the person manipulating the controls to see and avoid other air traffic or objects aloft or on the ground (part 107, § 107.3).

4.2.12 <u>Voluntary Consensus Standards Body</u>. Voluntary consensus standards bodies are domestic or international organizations that plan, develop, establish, or coordinate voluntary standards using agreed-upon procedures. A voluntary consensus standards body observes principles such as openness, balance of interest, and due process. These bodies may include nonprofit organizations, industry associations, accredited standards developers, professional and technical societies, committees, task forces, or working groups.

Table 4-1. Abbreviations/Acronyms Used in This AC

AAAM	Association for the Advancement of Automotive Medicine
AC	Advisory Circular
ACR	Airman Certification Representative
ACS	Airman Certification Standards
ACTS	Airman Certificate Testing Service
AD	Airworthiness Directive
ADM	Aeronautical Decision-Making
AELP	Aviation English Language Proficiency
AGL	Above Ground Level
AIM	Aeronautical Information Manual
AIS	Abbreviated Injury Scale
AKTR	Airman Knowledge Test Report
ASI	Aviation Safety Inspector
AST	Aviation Safety Technician
ATC	Air Traffic Control
ATO	Air Traffic Organization
AWC	Aviation Weather Center
C2	Command and Control
CFI	Certificated Flight Instructor
CFR	Code of Federal Regulations
CG	Center of Gravity
COA	Certificate of Waiver or Authorization
CoW	Certificate of Waiver
CRM	Crew Resource Management
CS	Control Station
DHS	Department of Homeland Security
DOC	Declaration of Compliance
DOT	Department of Transportation
DPE	Designated Pilot Examiner
EDL	Enhanced Driver's License

EID	Enhanced Identification Card
EMS	Emergency Medical Service
ETC	Enhanced Tribal Card
FAA	Federal Aviation Administration
FAASTeam	FAA Safety Team
FAST	Free and Secure Trade
FCC	Federal Communications Commission
FRIA	FAA-Recognized Identification Area
FSDO	Flight Standards District Office
FTN	FAA Tracking Number
GCS	Ground Control Station
GPS	Global Positioning System
IACRA	Integrated Airman Certification and Rating Application
ICA	Instructions for Continued Airworthiness
ICAO	International Civil Aviation Organization
INS	Immigration and Naturalization Service
KTC	Knowledge Testing Center
LOC	Loss of Control
METAR	Aviation Routine Weather Report
MMC	Merchant Mariner Credential
MOC	Means of Compliance
mph	Miles per Hour
MSL	Mean Sea Level
NAS	National Airspace System
NOTAM	Notice to Air Missions
NTIA	National Telecommunications and Information Administration
NTSB	National Transportation Safety Board
NWS	National Weather Service
PIC	Pilot in Command
PL	Public Law
RF	Radio Frequency
ROC	Regional Operations Center

sm	Statute Mile
TAF	Terminal Aerodrome Forecast
TFR	Temporary Flight Restriction
TSA	Transportation Security Administration
TWIC	Transportation Worker Identification Credential
UAS	Unmanned Aircraft System
U.S.C.	United States Code
USCIS	U.S. Citizenship and Immigration Services
VLOS	Visual Line of Sight
VO	Visual Observer
W&B	Weight and Balance
WINGS	Pilot Proficiency Program

4.3   Falsification, Reproduction, or Alteration. The FAA relies on information provided by owners and remote pilots of small UAS when it authorizes operations or when it has to make a compliance determination. Accordingly, the United States government may take appropriate action against a small UAS owner, operator, remote PIC, applicant for a DOC, or anyone else who fraudulently or knowingly provides false records or reports, or otherwise reproduces or alters any records, reports, or other information for fraudulent purposes. Such action could include the FAA's imposition of civil sanctions and the suspension or revocation of a certificate or waiver (§ 107.5).

4.4   Accident Reporting. The remote PIC of the small unmanned aircraft is required to report an accident to the FAA within 10 days if it meets any of the following thresholds:

1. At least serious injury to any person or any loss of consciousness. A serious injury is an injury that qualifies as Level 3 or higher on the Abbreviated Injury Scale (AIS) of the Association for the Advancement of Automotive Medicine (AAAM). The AIS is an anatomical scoring system that provides a means of ranking the severity of an injury and is widely used by emergency medical personnel. The FAA currently uses serious injury (AIS Level 3) as an injury threshold in other FAA regulations.

    AIS 3 Example: A person requires hospitalization, but the injury can fully heal (including, but not limited to, head trauma, broken bone(s), or laceration(s) to the skin that requires suturing).

2. Damage to any property, other than the small unmanned aircraft, if the cost is greater than $500 to repair or replace the property (whichever is lower).

    Example: A small unmanned aircraft damages a property with a fair market value of $200, and it would cost $600 to repair the damage. Because the fair market value is below $500, this accident is not required to be reported. Similarly, if the aircraft causes $200 worth of damage to property with a fair market value of $600, that accident is also not required to be reported because the repair cost is below $500 (§ 107.9).

4.4.1 <u>Submitting the Report</u>. The accident report must be made within 10 calendar-days of the operation that created the injury or damage. The report may be submitted to the appropriate FAA Regional Operations Center (ROC) electronically or by telephone. Electronic reporting can be completed at https://www.faa.gov/uas/. To make a report by phone, see Figure 4-1, FAA Regional Operations Centers Telephone List. Reports may also be made to the responsible Flight Standards office (refer to https://www.faa.gov/about/office_org/field_offices/fsdo/). The report should include the following information:

1. Small UAS remote PIC's name and contact information;

2. Small UAS remote PIC's FAA airman certificate number;

3. Small UAS registration number issued to the aircraft (FAA registration number);

4. Location of the accident;

5. Date of the accident;

6. Local time of the accident;

7. Whether any serious injury or fatality occurred;

8. Property damaged and extent of damage, if any or known; and

9. Description of what happened.

Figure 4-1. FAA Regional Operations Centers Telephone List

FAA REGIONAL OPERATIONS CENTERS	
LOCATION WHERE ACCIDENT OCCURRED:	**TELEPHONE:**
DC, DE, MD, NJ, NY, PA, WV, and VA	404-305-5150
AL, CT, FL, GA, KY, MA, ME, MS, NC, NH, PR, RI, SC, TN, VI, and VT	404-305-5156
AK, AS, AZ, CA, CO, GU, HI, ID, MP, MT, NV, OR, UT, WA, and WY	425-227-1999
AR, IA, IL, IN, KS, LA, MI, MN, MO, ND, NE, NM, OH, OK, SD, TX, and WI	817-222-5006

4.4.2 <u>National Transportation Safety Board (NTSB) Reporting</u>. In addition to the report submitted to the ROC, and in accordance with the criteria established by the NTSB, certain small unmanned aircraft accidents must also be reported to the NTSB. NTSB's regulations, codified at 49 CFR part 830, require immediate notification when an aircraft accident occurs. NTSB regulations define an "unmanned aircraft accident" as an occurrence associated with the operation of any public or civil UAS that takes place between the time that the system is activated with the purpose of flight and the time that the system is deactivated at the conclusion of its mission, in which any person suffers death or serious injury, or the aircraft has a maximum gross takeoff weight of 300 pounds or greater and sustains substantial damage. NTSB regulations contain specific definitions for "serious injury" and "substantial damage" (49 CFR part 830, § 830.2). For more information, visit https://www.ntsb.gov.

CHAPTER 5. PART 107 SUBPART B, OPERATING RULES (SMALL UAS)

5.1 Applicability. This chapter provides guidance regarding small unmanned aircraft operating limitations and the responsibilities of the remote pilot in command (PIC), person manipulating the controls, visual observer (VO), and anyone else who may directly participate in the small UAS operation. A person is a direct participant in the small UAS operation if their involvement is necessary for the safe operation of the small UAS.

5.2 Aircraft Operation. Just like a manned-aircraft PIC, the remote PIC of a small unmanned aircraft is directly responsible for and is the final authority for the safe operation of the small unmanned aircraft (§ 107.19). Additionally, a person manipulating the controls (who is not the remote PIC) can participate in flight operations under certain conditions. It is important to note that a person may not operate or act as a remote PIC or VO in the operation of more than one small unmanned aircraft at the same time (§ 107.35). The following items describe the requirements for both a remote PIC and a person manipulating the controls.

5.2.1 Remote PIC. A person acting as a remote PIC of a small UAS under part 107 must obtain a Remote Pilot Certificate with a small UAS rating issued by the FAA prior to small UAS operation (§ 107.12). The remote PIC must have, in that person's physical possession and readily accessible, this certificate and personal identification during flight operations (§§ 107.7 and 107.67(b)(1) through (3)). Guidance regarding remote pilot certification is found in Chapter 6, Part 107 Subpart C, Remote Pilot Certification.

5.2.1.1 Part 107 permits transfer of control of a small UAS between certificated remote pilots. Two or more certificated remote pilots transferring operational control (i.e., the remote PIC designation) to each other may do so only if they are both capable of maintaining Visual Line of Sight (VLOS) of the small unmanned aircraft without loss of control (LOC). One remote pilot may be designated the remote PIC at the beginning of the operation, and at some point in the operation another remote pilot may take over as remote PIC by positively communicating the transfer of control. The remote PIC assuming control of the small UAS maintains responsibility for the safe operation of the small UAS.

5.2.2 Person Manipulating the Flight Controls. A person who does not hold a Remote Pilot Certificate or a remote pilot who has not met the recurrent training requirements of part 107 may operate the small UAS under part 107, as long as they are directly supervised by a remote PIC and the remote PIC has the ability to take immediate, direct control of the small UAS. This ability is necessary to ensure the remote PIC can quickly address any hazardous situation. The ability of the remote PIC to take over the flight controls immediately could be achieved by using a number of different methods. The operation could involve a "buddy box" type system that uses two control stations (CS): one for the person manipulating the flight controls and one for the remote PIC that allows the remote PIC to override the other CS and immediately take direct control of the small unmanned aircraft (§ 107.19). Another method could involve the remote PIC standing close enough to the person manipulating the flight controls so that they would be able to physically take over the CS from the other person. Another method could employ the use of an automation system where the remote PIC could immediately engage that system to put the small unmanned aircraft in a pre-programmed "safe" mode such as a hover, a holding pattern, or "return home."

5.2.3 <u>Automated Operations</u>. An automated operation is generally considered an operation in which the remote pilot inputs a flight plan into the CS, which sends the flight plan to the autopilot on board the small unmanned aircraft. During automated flight, flight control inputs are made by components on board the aircraft, not from a CS. If the remote PIC loses the control link to the small unmanned aircraft, the aircraft would continue to fly the programmed mission/return home to land. During automated flight, the remote PIC must have the ability to change routing/altitude or command the aircraft to land immediately. The ability to direct the small unmanned aircraft may be through manual manipulation of the flight controls or through commands using automation.

    5.2.3.1   The remote PIC must retain the ability to direct the small unmanned aircraft to ensure compliance with the requirements of part 107. The remote PIC may transmit a command for the automated aircraft to climb, descend, land now, proceed to a new waypoint, enter an orbit pattern, or return to home. Any of these methods may be used to avoid a hazard or give right-of-way.

    5.2.3.2   The use of automation does not allow a person to operate more than one small unmanned aircraft simultaneously (§ 107.35).

5.3 **Aeronautical Decision-Making (ADM) and Crew Resource Management (CRM).** ADM is a systematic approach to the mental process used by pilots to determine consistently the best course of action in response to a given set of circumstances. A remote PIC uses many different resources to safely operate a small unmanned aircraft and needs to be able to manage these resources effectively. CRM is a component of ADM, in which the pilot of a small unmanned aircraft makes effective use of all available resources: human resources, hardware, and information. Many remote pilots operating under part 107 may use a VO, oversee other persons manipulating the controls of the small UAS, or any other person with whom the remote PIC may interact to ensure safe operations. Therefore, a remote PIC must be able to function in a team environment and maximize team performance. This skill set includes situational awareness, proper allocation of tasks to individuals, avoidance of work overloads for themselves and in others, and effectively communicating with other members of the crew, such as VOs and persons manipulating the controls of a small unmanned aircraft. Appendix <u>A</u>, Risk Assessment Tools, contains expanded information on ADM and CRM, as well as sample risk assessment tools to aid in identifying hazards and mitigating risks.

5.4 **Aircraft Registration.** A small unmanned aircraft must be registered, in accordance with part 47 or part 48, prior to operating under part 107. Part 48 is the regulation that establishes the streamlined online registration option for small unmanned aircraft that will be operated only within the territorial limits of the United States. The online registration website is https://faadronezone.faa.gov/. Guidance regarding small

unmanned aircraft registration and marking may be found at
https://www.faa.gov/licenses_certificates/aircraft_certification/aircraft_registry/.
Alternatively, small unmanned aircraft owners or operators can elect to register under
part 47 in the same manner as manned aircraft.

5.4.1 Registration and Permit for Foreign-Owned and Operated Small UAS. If small UAS
operations involve the use of foreign civil aircraft, the operator would need to obtain a
Foreign Aircraft Permit pursuant to 14 CFR part 375, as described in § 375.41, before
conducting any commercial air operations under this authority. Foreign civil aircraft
means (a) an aircraft of foreign registry that is not part of the armed forces of a foreign
nation, or (b) a U.S.-registered aircraft owned, controlled, or operated by persons who are
not citizens or permanent residents of the United States. Application instructions are
specified in § 375.43. Applications should be submitted by electronic mail to the
Department of Transportation (DOT) Office of International Aviation, Foreign
Air Carrier Licensing Division at https://cms.dot.gov/policy/aviation-policy/licensing/for
eign-carriers. Foreign-owned and operated small UAS must be registered, as provided for
under part 47 or part 48, including submission of an Affidavit of Ownership for
Unmanned Aircraft, if necessary. Additional information can be obtained at
https://www.faa.gov/licenses_certificates/aircraft_certification/aircraft_registry/UA/.
(Refer to Title 49 of the United States Code (49 U.S.C.) § 44101(b)(1) for exceptions.)

5.5 **Small Unmanned Aircraft Maintenance, Inspections, and Condition for Safe
Operation.** A small unmanned aircraft must be maintained in a condition for safe
operation. Prior to flight, the remote PIC is responsible for conducting a check of the
small unmanned aircraft to verify it is actually in a condition for safe operation
(§ 107.15). Guidance regarding how to determine that a small unmanned aircraft is in a
condition for safe operation is found in Chapter 7, Small Unmanned Aircraft
Maintenance and Inspection.

5.6 **Medical Condition.** Being able to operate the small unmanned aircraft safely relies on,
among other things, the physical and mental capabilities of the remote PIC, person
manipulating the controls, VO, and any other direct participant in the small UAS
operation. Though the person manipulating the controls of a small unmanned aircraft and
VO are not required to obtain an airman medical certificate, they cannot participate in the
operation of a small UAS if they know or have reason to know that they have a physical
or mental condition that could interfere with the safe operation of the small UAS
(§ 107.17).

5.6.1 Physical or Mental Incapacitations. Obvious examples of physical or mental
incapacitations that could render a remote PIC, person manipulating the controls, or VO
incapable of performing their small UAS operational duties include, but are not limited
to, such things as:

1. The temporary or permanent loss of the dexterity necessary to operate the CS to
    control the small unmanned aircraft safely.

2. The inability to maintain the required "see and avoid" vigilance due to blurred vision.

3. The inability to maintain proper situational awareness of the small unmanned aircraft operations due to illness and/or medication(s), such as after taking medications that caution against driving or operating heavy machinery.

4. A debilitating physical condition, such as a migraine headache or moderate or severe body ache(s) or pain(s) that would render the remote PIC, person manipulating the controls, or VO unable to perform small UAS operational duties.

5. A hearing or speaking impairment that would inhibit the remote PIC, person manipulating the controls, or VO from effectively communicating with each other. In such a situation, the remote PIC must ensure they implement an alternative means of effective communication. For example, a person who is hearing impaired may be able to use sign language to communicate effectively.

5.7 Civil Twilight and Operations at Night. Night is defined in § 1.1 as the time between the end of evening civil twilight and the beginning of morning civil twilight, as published in The Air Almanac, converted to local time. In the continental United States, evening civil twilight is the period of sunset until 30 minutes after sunset and morning civil twilight is the period of 30 minutes prior to sunrise until sunrise. In Alaska, the definition of civil twilight differs and is described in The Air Almanac. The Air Almanac provides tables to determine sunrise and sunset at various latitudes. These tables can also be downloaded from the Naval Observatory and customized for a particular location. The link for the Naval Observatory is https://www.usno.navy.mil/search?SearchableText=air+almanac+.

5.7.1 <u>Civil Twilight Operations</u>. When small UAS operations occur during civil twilight, the small unmanned aircraft must be equipped with anti-collision lighting visible for at least 3 statute miles (sm). However, the remote PIC may reduce the visible distance of the lighting to less than 3 sm during flight if they have determined that it would be in the interest of safety to do so. For more information on this determination, see paragraph 5.7.2.2.

5.7.2 <u>Operations at Night</u>. Small UAS operations at night may occur only under the two risk mitigation measures listed in § 107.29. First, the remote PIC must have completed either an initial knowledge test or recurrent training that have been updated to include night operations. Second, the small unmanned aircraft must have lighted anti-collision lighting that is visible for at least 3 sm. The remote pilot may rely upon manufacturer statements indicating the anti-collision lighting is visible for 3 sm. However, the remote pilot ultimately remains responsible for verifying that anti-collision lighting is operational, visible for 3 sm, and has a flash rate sufficient to avoid a collision at the operating location.

5.7.2.1 A certificated remote pilot receives night operations privileges and may operate at night only after completing either a knowledge test that contains questions on night physiology and night visual illusions, or through completion of recurrent training. The recurrent training contains the topics of night physiology and night visual illusions. Chapter 6 provides a detailed explanation of both paths for night operations privileges.

5.7.2.2 As is the case for civil twilight operations, the small unmanned aircraft must be equipped with anti-collision lighting that is visible for at least 3 sm. However, the remote PIC may reduce the intensity of the light if the remote PIC determines it is in the interest of safety to do so. For example, a bright light or a bright strobe light on the small unmanned aircraft in very close proximity to the remote pilot could cause the remote pilot to lose the ability to observe the small unmanned aircraft's location, speed, attitude, or altitude with accuracy. The remote pilot maintains the discretion to reduce the intensity of the anti-collision lighting when they determine it would be in the best interest of safety to do so. Discretion is an important component of § 107.19, which states that the remote PIC is directly responsible for the operation of the small unmanned aircraft. The remote PIC must ensure the operation of the small unmanned aircraft complies with all regulations of part 107. This includes the requirement to maintain the capability of visually observing the small unmanned aircraft. Section 107.29 does not require small unmanned aircraft operating during the day to have illuminated small unmanned aircraft anti-collision lighting. Lighting is generally not effective for mitigating risk of collision during daytime operations. Remote pilots may exercise their discretion, however, and elect to have lighting on during all daytime operations.

5.7.2.3 A remote PIC or operator may request a waiver of the anti-collision lighting requirement for operations at night and during civil twilight. The process for requesting a waiver is two-fold: the requester must (1) fully describe the proposed operation, and (2) establish the operation can be safely conducted under the terms of a Certificate of Waiver (CoW). Paragraph 5.20 below describes the application process for waivers.

5.8 Operations Over Open-Air Assemblies of Persons. Remote pilots are prohibited from operating a small unmanned aircraft as a Category 1, 2, or 4 operation in sustained flight over open-air assemblies, unless the operation meets the requirements of 14 CFR part 89, § 89.110 or § 89.115(a). Category 3 operations are not allowed over an open-air assembly of persons.

Note: See paragraphs 8.3.2 and 8.3.6.4 for more information regarding open-air assemblies of persons.

5.9 VLOS Aircraft Operation. The remote PIC and person manipulating the controls must be able to see the small unmanned aircraft at all times during flight (§ 107.31). The small unmanned aircraft must be operated closely enough to ensure visibility requirements are met during small UAS operations. This requirement also applies to the VO, if used, during the aircraft operation. The person maintaining VLOS may have brief moments in which they are not looking directly at or cannot see the small unmanned aircraft, but still retain the capability to see the small unmanned aircraft or quickly maneuver it back to VLOS. These moments may be necessary for the remote PIC to look at the controller to determine remaining battery life or for operational awareness. Should the remote PIC or person manipulating the controls lose VLOS of the small unmanned aircraft, they must regain VLOS as soon as practicable. Even though the remote PIC may briefly lose sight of the small unmanned aircraft, the remote PIC always has the see-and-avoid responsibilities set out in §§ 107.31 and 107.37. The circumstances that may prevent a remote PIC from fulfilling those responsibilities will vary, depending on factors such as the type of small UAS, the operational environment, and distance between the remote PIC and the small unmanned aircraft. For this reason, no specific time interval exists in which interruption of VLOS is permissible, as it would have the effect of potentially allowing a hazardous interruption of the operation. If the remote PIC cannot regain VLOS, the remote PIC or person manipulating the controls should follow pre-determined procedures for the loss of VLOS. The capabilities of the small UAS will govern the remote PIC's determination as to the appropriate course of action. For example, the remote PIC may need to land the small unmanned aircraft immediately, enter hover mode, or employ a return-to-home sequence. The VLOS requirement does not prohibit actions such as scanning the airspace or briefly looking down at the small unmanned aircraft CS.

5.9.1   Unaided Vision. VLOS must be accomplished and maintained by unaided vision, except vision that is corrected by the use of eyeglasses (spectacles) or contact lenses. Vision aids, such as binoculars, may be used only momentarily to enhance situational awareness. For example, the remote PIC, person manipulating the controls, or VO may use vision aids to avoid inadvertently flying over persons or conflicting with other aircraft. First person view devices may be used during operations, but do not satisfy the VLOS requirement.

5.9.2   VO. The use of a VO is optional. The remote PIC may choose to use a VO to supplement situational awareness and VLOS. Although the remote PIC and person manipulating the controls must maintain the capability to see the small unmanned aircraft, using one or more VOs allows the remote PIC and person manipulating the controls to conduct other mission-critical duties (such as checking displays) while still ensuring situational awareness of the small unmanned aircraft. The VO must be able to communicate effectively with regard to the following:

- The small unmanned aircraft location, attitude, altitude, and direction of flight;

- The position of other aircraft or hazards in the airspace; and

- The determination that the small unmanned aircraft does not endanger the life or property of another (§ 107.33).

5.9.2.1   To ensure the VO can carry out their duties, the remote PIC must ensure the VO is positioned in a location where the VO is able to see the small unmanned aircraft sufficiently to maintain VLOS. The remote PIC can do this by specifying the location of the VO. The FAA also requires the remote PIC and VO coordinate to (1) scan the airspace where the small unmanned aircraft is operating for any potential collision hazard, and (2) maintain awareness of the position of the small unmanned aircraft through direct visual observation (§ 107.33). The remote PIC and VO would accomplish this by the VO communicating to the remote PIC and person manipulating the controls the flight status of the small unmanned aircraft and any collision hazards which may enter the area of operation, so that the remote PIC or person manipulating the controls can take appropriate action. The VO's visual observation of the small unmanned aircraft and surrounding airspace would enable the VO to inform the remote PIC of the status.

5.9.2.2 To make this communication possible, the remote PIC, person manipulating the controls, and VO must work out a method of effective communication that does not create a distraction. Such a means of communication entails the constant ability to understand one another. The communication method must be determined prior to operation. Effective communication would permit the use of communication-assisting devices, such as a handheld radio, to facilitate communication from a distance.

5.9.3 VLOS at Night. Prior to a small UAS operation at night, the remote PIC should ensure they will be able to keep the small unmanned aircraft within the intended area of operation and within VLOS for the duration of the operation. In almost all cases involving operations at night, the remote PIC may need to restrict the operational area of the small unmanned aircraft. Reduced lighting and contrast at night may make it difficult for remote pilots to fulfill the requirements of § 107.31(a), requiring remote pilots to maintain the capability of visually discerning the location, attitude, altitude, and direction of the flight of the aircraft. A remote pilot cannot solely rely on the small unmanned aircraft's anti-collision lighting, Ground Control Station (GCS) telemetry data displays, or a combination of the two for compliance with § 107.31.

5.10 Operation Near Airports, in Certain Airspace, in Prohibited or Restricted Areas, or in the Proximity of Certain Areas Designated by a Notice to Air Missions (NOTAM). Small unmanned aircraft may operate in controlled or uncontrolled airspace. Operations in Class B, Class C, or Class D airspace, or within the lateral boundaries of the surface area of Class E airspace designated for an airport, are not permitted unless that person has prior authorization from air traffic control (ATC) (§ 107.41). Information concerning the current authorization process is available at https://www.faa.gov/uas/. The remote PIC must understand airspace classifications and requirements. Failure to do so could be contrary to part 107 regulations and may potentially have an adverse effect on the safety of operations. Small UAS operating under part 107 may not be subject to part 91 requirements, because the equipage and communications requirements outlined in part 91 were designed to provide safety and efficiency in the National Airspace System (NAS). ATC authorizations may depend on operational parameters similar to those found in part 91. The FAA has the authority to approve or deny aircraft operations based on traffic density, controller workload, communication issues, or any other type of operation that could potentially impact the safe and expeditious flow of air traffic in that airspace.

5.10.1 Small Unmanned Aircraft Operations Near an Airport—Notification and Permissions. Unless the flight is conducted within controlled airspace, no notification or authorization is necessary to operate a small unmanned aircraft at or near an airport. When operating in the vicinity of an airport, the remote PIC must be aware of and avoid all traffic patterns and approach corridors to runways and landing areas. The remote PIC must avoid operating in any area in which the presence of the small UAS may interfere with operations at the airport, such as approach corridors, taxiways, runways, or helipads (§ 107.43). The remote PIC must yield right-of-way to all other aircraft, including aircraft operating on the surface of the airport (§ 107.43).

5.10.1.1   Remote PICs are prohibited from operating a small unmanned aircraft in a manner that interferes with operations and traffic patterns at airports, heliports, and seaplane bases (§ 107.43). Small unmanned aircraft must always yield right-of-way to a manned aircraft. A manned aircraft may alter its flightpath, delay its landing, or take off in order to avoid a small unmanned aircraft that may present a potential conflict or otherwise affect the safe outcome of the flight. A small unmanned aircraft hovering 200 feet above a runway may cause a manned aircraft holding short of the runway to delay takeoff, or a manned aircraft on the downwind leg of the pattern to delay landing. While the small unmanned aircraft in this scenario would not present an immediate traffic conflict to the aircraft on the downwind leg of the traffic pattern or to the aircraft intending to take off, nor would it violate the right-of-way provision of § 107.37(a), the small unmanned aircraft would have interfered with the operations of the traffic pattern at an airport.

5.10.1.2   In order to avoid interfering with operations in a traffic pattern, remote PICs should avoid operating in the traffic pattern or published approach corridors used by manned aircraft. When operational necessity requires the remote PIC to operate at an airport in uncontrolled airspace, the remote PIC should operate the small unmanned aircraft in such a way that the manned aircraft pilot does not need to alter their flightpath in the traffic pattern or on a published instrument approach in order to avoid a potential collision.

5.10.2   Air Traffic Organization (ATO). When receiving requests for authorization to operate in controlled airspace, ATO does not approve or deny small unmanned aircraft operations on the basis of equipage that exceeds the part 107 requirements. Additional equipage and technologies, such as geo-fencing, have not been certified by the FAA and need to be examined on a case-by-case basis in order for the FAA to determine their reliability and functionality. Additionally, requiring staff from ATO to review equipage would place a burden on ATO and detract from other duties. Instead of seeking an authorization, a remote pilot who wishes to operate in controlled airspace because the remote pilot can demonstrate mitigations through equipage may do so by applying for a CoW (see paragraph 5.20).

5.10.3   Temporary Flight Restrictions (TFR). Certain TFRs may be imposed by way of a NOTAM. Refer to https://www.1800wxbrief.com. The remote PIC must check for NOTAMs before each flight to determine whether any airspace restrictions apply to the operation.

5.10.4   <u>Type of Airspace</u>. Remote PICs must also be aware of the type of airspace in which they will be operating their small unmanned aircraft. Referring to the B4UFly app or a current aeronautical chart (refer to https://www.faa.gov/air_traffic/flight_info/aeronav/digital_products/) of the intended operating area will aid the small unmanned aircraft remote PIC's decision making regarding operations in the NAS.

5.11   Preflight Familiarization, Inspection, and Actions for Aircraft Operation. The remote PIC must complete a preflight familiarization, inspection, and other actions, such as crewmember briefings, prior to beginning flight operations (§ 107.49). The FAA has produced many publications providing in-depth information on topics such as aviation weather, aircraft loading and performance, emergency procedures, risk mitigation, ADM, and airspace, which should all be considered prior to operations (see Appendix <u>E</u>, Sample Preflight Assessment and Inspection Checklist). Additionally, all remote pilots are encouraged to review FAA publications (see paragraph <u>2.3</u>).

5.11.1   <u>Prior to Flight</u>. The remote PIC must:

1. Conduct an assessment of the operating environment. The assessment must include at least the following:

   - Local weather conditions;

   - Local airspace and any flight restrictions;

   - The location of persons and moving vehicles not directly participating in the operation, and property on the surface;

   - If conducting operations over people or moving vehicles, ensure their small unmanned aircraft is eligible for the category or categories of operations (see Chapter <u>8</u>);

   - Consider the potential for persons and moving vehicles not directly participating in operations entering the operational area for the duration of the operation;

   - Consider whether the operation will be conducted over an open-air assembly of persons; and

   - Other ground hazards.

   Note: Remote pilots are prohibited from operating a small unmanned aircraft as a Category 1, 2, or 4 operation in sustained flight over open-air assemblies unless the operation meets the requirements of § 89.110 or § 89.115(a).

2. Ensure all persons directly participating in the small UAS operation are informed about the following:

   - Operating conditions;

   - Emergency procedures;

- Contingency procedures, including those for persons or moving vehicles not directly participating in the operation that enter the operational area;

- Roles and responsibilities of each person participating in the operation; and

- Potential hazards.

3. Ensure all control links between the CS and the small unmanned aircraft are working properly. Before each flight, the remote PIC must determine the small unmanned aircraft flight control surfaces necessary for the safety of flight are moving correctly through the manipulation of the small unmanned aircraft CS. If the remote PIC observes that one or more of the control surfaces are not responding correctly to CS inputs, then the remote PIC may not conduct flight operations until correct movement of all flight control surface(s) is established.

4. Ensure sufficient power exists to continue controlled flight operations to a normal landing. This can be accomplished by following the small UAS manufacturer's operating manual power consumption tables. Another method would be to include a system on the small UAS that detects power levels and alerts the remote pilot when remaining aircraft power is diminishing to a level that is inadequate for continued flight operation.

5. Ensure the small unmanned aircraft anti-collision light(s) function(s) properly prior to any flight that will occur during civil twilight or at night. The remote PIC must also consider, during their preflight check, whether the anti-collision light(s) could reduce the amount of power available to the small unmanned aircraft. The remote PIC may need to reduce the planned duration of the small unmanned aircraft operation to ensure sufficient power exists to maintain the illuminated anti-collision light(s) and to ensure sufficient power exists for the small unmanned aircraft to proceed to a normal landing.

6. Ensure any object attached or carried by the small unmanned aircraft is secure and does not adversely affect the flight characteristics or controllability of the aircraft.

7. Ensure all necessary documentation is available for inspection, including the remote PIC's Remote Pilot Certificate, identification, aircraft registration, and CoW, if applicable (§ 107.7).

5.11.2 <u>Safety Risk Assessment</u>. These preflight familiarizations, inspections, and actions can be accomplished as part of an overall safety risk assessment. The FAA encourages the remote PIC to conduct the overall safety risk assessment as a method of compliance with the restriction on operating over any person who is not directly involved in the operation, unless the small unmanned aircraft is eligible for an operation over people in accordance with part 107 subpart D. The safety risk assessment also assists with ensuring the small unmanned aircraft will remain clear of other aircraft. Appendix <u>A</u> provides additional guidance on how to conduct an overall safety risk assessment.

5.12   Operating Limitations for Small Unmanned Aircraft. Operations of the small unmanned aircraft must comply with the following limitations:

- Cannot be flown faster than a groundspeed of 87 knots (100 miles per hour (mph));

- Cannot be flown higher than 400 feet above ground level (AGL), unless flown within a 400-foot radius of a structure and does not fly higher than 400 feet above the structure's immediate uppermost limit;

- Minimum visibility, as observed from the location of the CS, may not be less than 3 sm; and

- Minimum distance from clouds being no less than 500 feet below a cloud and no less than 2,000 feet horizontally from the cloud (§ 107.51).

Note: These operating limitations are intended, among other things, to support the remote pilot's ability to identify hazardous conditions relating to encroaching aircraft or persons on the ground, and to take appropriate actions to maintain safety.

5.12.1   Determining Groundspeed. Many different types of small unmanned aircraft and different ways to determine groundspeed exist. This guidance will only touch on some of the possible means for the remote PIC to ensure the small unmanned aircraft does not exceed a groundspeed of 87 knots during flight operations. Examples of methods to ensure compliance with this limitation are:

- Installing a Global Positioning System (GPS) device on the small unmanned aircraft that reports groundspeed information to the remote pilot, allowing the remote pilot to determine the wind direction and speed and calculate the small unmanned aircraft airspeed for a given direction of flight;

- Timing the groundspeed of the small unmanned aircraft when it is flown between two or more fixed points, considering wind speed and direction between each point, then noting the power settings of the small unmanned aircraft to operate at or less than 87 knots groundspeed; or

- Using the small unmanned aircraft's manufacturer design limitations (e.g., installed groundspeed limiters).

5.12.2   Determining Altitude. In order to comply with the maximum altitude requirements of part 107, a remote pilot may determine altitude by:

- Installing a calibrated altitude reporting device on the small unmanned aircraft that reports the small unmanned aircraft altitude above mean sea level (MSL) to the remote pilot, who subtracts the MSL elevation of the CS from the small unmanned aircraft reported MSL altitude to determine the small unmanned aircraft AGL altitude above the terrain or structure;

- Installing a GPS device on the small unmanned aircraft that has the capability of reporting MSL altitude to the remote pilot;

- Having the remote pilot and VO pace off 400 feet from the small unmanned aircraft while it is on the ground to get a visual perspective of distance so that the remote pilot and VO can recognize and maintain that visual perspective (or closer) when the small unmanned aircraft is in flight; or

- Using the known height of local rising terrain and/or structures as a reference.

5.12.3 <u>Visibility and Distance from Clouds</u>. The remote PIC must determine that the visibility from the CS is at least 3 sm and that the small unmanned aircraft maintains at least 500 feet below clouds and at least 2,000 feet horizontally from clouds. Obtaining local aviation weather reports that include current and forecast weather conditions is one means of determining visibility and cloud clearance. If there is more than one local aviation reporting station near the operating area, the remote PIC should choose the closest one that is most representative of the terrain surrounding the operating area. If local aviation weather reports are not available, the remote PIC cannot operate the small unmanned aircraft until they are able to determine the required visibility and cloud clearances by other reliable means. The small unmanned aircraft cannot be operated above any cloud, and there cannot be obstructions to visibility, such as smoke or a cloud, between the small unmanned aircraft and the remote PIC (§ 107.39).

5.13 **Remaining Clear of Other Aircraft.** A remote PIC has a responsibility to operate the small unmanned aircraft so that it remains clear of and yields to all other aircraft (§ 107.37). This is traditionally referred to as "see and avoid." To satisfy this responsibility, the remote PIC must know the location and flightpath of their small unmanned aircraft at all times. The remote PIC must be aware of other aircraft, persons, and property in the vicinity of the operating area, and maneuver the small unmanned aircraft to avoid collision. The remote PIC must take action to ensure other aircraft will not need to maneuver to avoid colliding with the small unmanned aircraft.

5.14 **Operations from Moving Vehicles.** Part 107 permits operation of a small unmanned aircraft from a moving land or water-borne vehicle over a sparsely-populated area. However, operation from a moving aircraft is prohibited. Additionally, small unmanned aircraft transporting another person's property for compensation or hire may not be operated from any moving vehicle (§ 107.25).

5.14.1 <u>Waiving the Sparsely-Populated Area Provision</u>. Although the regulation states that operations from a moving vehicle may only be conducted over a sparsely-populated area, this provision may be waived (§§ 107.200 and 107.205). The operation is subject to the same restrictions that apply to all other part 107 operations. The remote PIC operating from a moving vehicle is still required to maintain VLOS. The remote PIC is also responsible for ensuring that no person is subject to undue risk as a result of LOC of the small unmanned aircraft for any reason. If a VO is not located in the same vehicle as the remote PIC, the VO and remote PIC must still maintain effective communication.

5.14.2 <u>Applicable Laws</u>. Other laws, such as State and local traffic laws, may apply to a person driving a vehicle and operating an unmanned aircraft from the vehicle. When operating a small UAS from a moving vehicle, the FAA emphasizes that people involved in the operation are responsible for complying with applicable State and local laws as well as FAA regulations.

5.15   Transportation of Property. Part 107 permits transportation of property by small unmanned aircraft for compensation or hire. These operations must be conducted within a confined area and in compliance with the operating restrictions of part 107. When transporting property, the transport must occur wholly within the bounds of a single State.

5.15.1 <u>Limitations</u>. As with other operations in part 107, small UAS operations involving the transport of property must be conducted within VLOS of the remote pilot. While the VLOS limitation can be waived for some operations under the rule, it cannot for transportation of property. Additionally, part 107 does not allow the operation of a small UAS from a moving vehicle or aircraft if the small unmanned aircraft is being used to transport property for compensation or hire. This limitation cannot be waived. The maximum total weight of the small unmanned aircraft (including any property being transported) is limited to under 55 pounds. Other provisions of part 107 require the remote pilot to know the small unmanned aircraft's location; to determine the small unmanned aircraft's attitude, altitude, and direction; to yield the right-of-way to other aircraft; and to maintain the ability to see and avoid other aircraft.

5.15.2 <u>Hazardous Materials</u>. Section 107.36 prohibits the carriage of hazardous materials by small unmanned aircraft. The carriage of any hazardous material on a small unmanned aircraft may only occur if the operator holds an exemption that permits such carriage. Title 14 CFR part 11 applies to petitions for exemption.

5.16   Operations While Impaired. Part 107 does not allow operation of a small UAS if the remote PIC, person manipulating the controls, or VO is unable to carry out their responsibilities safely (§ 107.27). It is the remote PIC's responsibility to ensure all crewmembers are not impaired while participating in the operation. While drug and alcohol use are known to impair judgment, certain over-the-counter medications and medical conditions could also affect the ability to operate a small unmanned aircraft safely. For example, certain antihistamines and decongestants may cause drowsiness. Additionally, part 107 prohibits a person from serving as a remote PIC, VO, or other crewmember, or manipulating the controls, if they:

- Consumed any alcoholic beverage within the preceding 8 hours;

- Are under the influence of alcohol;

- Have a blood alcohol concentration of .04 percent or greater; or

- Are using a drug that affects the person's mental or physical capabilities (§ 91.17).

5.16.1 <u>Medical Conditions</u>. Certain medical conditions, such as epilepsy, may also create a risk to operations. It is the responsibility of remote PICs to determine that their medical condition is under control and they can safely conduct a small UAS operation.

5.17   **Remote Identification of Unmanned Aircraft Systems.** Remote identification requirements are contained in part 89. The information contained in this AC covers the remote identification operational requirements that are relevant to all part 107 operators. Additional information related to remote identification is available in the following ACs:

- AC 89-1, Means of Compliance Process for Remote Identification of Unmanned Aircraft.

- AC 89-2, Declaration of Compliance Process for Remote Identification of Unmanned Aircraft.

5.17.1   After September 16, 2023, most small unmanned aircraft that are registered or required to be registered must comply with remote identification requirements. The serial number of a standard remote identification unmanned aircraft, or of the remote identification broadcast module, if one is installed on the unmanned aircraft, must be listed on the Certificate of Aircraft Registration. The serial number may only be listed on one Certificate of Aircraft Registration at a time. The remote identification broadcast module may be moved from one unmanned aircraft operated under part 107 to another, but the serial number must also be moved from the first aircraft's Certificate of Aircraft Registration to the second aircraft's certificate prior to operation. Small unmanned aircraft that are not required to be registered under part 48, such as those where the unmanned aircraft weighs 0.55 pounds or less, must comply with remote identification requirements when operated under any operating part for which registration is required. Remote identification provides data regarding the location and identification of small unmanned aircraft operating in the NAS. It also provides airspace awareness to the FAA, national security agencies, and law enforcement entities, which can be used to distinguish compliant airspace users from those potentially posing a safety or security risk. A list of unmanned aircraft by make and model that are compliant with remote identification will be found at https://www.faa.gov/uas, when developed.

5.17.2   Standard remote identification unmanned aircraft broadcast certain message elements over radio frequency (RF) spectrum. These message elements include: Unmanned Aircraft Identification (either the unmanned aircraft's serial number or session ID); latitude, longitude, and geometric altitude of both the CS and the unmanned aircraft; the velocity of the unmanned aircraft (including horizontal and vertical speed and direction); a time mark; and an emergency status code (§ 89.110).

5.17.3   Small unmanned aircraft without remote identification. Small unmanned aircraft that are not standard remote identification unmanned aircraft may operate in one of two ways: the small unmanned aircraft may be equipped with a remote identification broadcast module, or the small unmanned aircraft may be operated within an FAA-recognized identification area (FRIA) (§ 89.115).

5.17.3.1   Unmanned aircraft equipped with remote identification modules may be integrated by the manufacturer (e.g., if a manufacturer upgraded or retrofit the aircraft) or a standalone broadcast module installed by the user secured to the unmanned aircraft prior to takeoff. The remote identification broadcast module broadcasts certain message elements directly from the unmanned aircraft over RF spectrum. These message elements include: the Unmanned Aircraft Identification, the unmanned aircraft's serial number; latitude, longitude, and geometric altitude of the unmanned aircraft; latitude, longitude, and geometric altitude of the takeoff location; the velocity of the unmanned aircraft (including horizontal and vertical speed and direction); and a time mark. Small unmanned aircraft using a remote identification broadcast module must be operated within VLOS (§ 89.115(a)).

5.17.3.2   A person operating a small unmanned aircraft that is not a standard remote identification unmanned aircraft may also operate within VLOS within a FRIA, regardless of the type of operation conducted (e.g., part 91, 107, or other). You will be able to access a list of FRIAs at https://www.faa.gov/uas when available (§ 89.115).

5.18   In-Flight Emergency. An in-flight emergency is an unexpected and unforeseen serious occurrence or situation that requires urgent, prompt action. In the case of an in-flight emergency, the remote PIC is permitted to deviate from any rule of part 107 to the extent necessary to respond to that emergency. A remote PIC who exercises this emergency power is required, upon the FAA's request, to send a written report to the FAA explaining the deviation. Emergency action should be taken in such a way as to minimize injury or damage to property (§ 107.21).

5.19   Careless or Reckless Operation. As with manned aircraft, remote PICs are prohibited from engaging in a careless or reckless operation (§ 107.23). Because small UAS have additional operating considerations that are not present in manned aircraft operations, additional activity may amount to careless or reckless operation if conducted using a small UAS. For example, careless or reckless operation may consist of failure to consider weather conditions near structures, trees, or rolling terrain when operating in a densely populated area.

5.20   Certificate of Waiver. Part 107 includes the option to apply for a CoW. This CoW will allow a small UAS operation to deviate from certain provisions of part 107 if the Administrator finds that the proposed operation can be safely conducted under the terms of that CoW (§ 107.200). A list of the sections of part 107 subject to waiver are listed below:

- Section 107.25: Operation from a moving vehicle or aircraft.
- Section 107.29(a)(2) and (b): Anti-collision light required for operations at night and during periods of civil twilight.
- Section 107.31: Visual line of sight aircraft operation. However, no waiver of this provision will be issued to allow the carriage of property of another by aircraft for compensation or hire.
- Section 107.33: Visual observer.
- Section 107.35: Operation of multiple small unmanned aircraft systems.
- Section 107.37(a): Yielding the right-of-way.

- Section 107.39: Operation over people.

- Section 107.41: Operation in certain airspace.

- Section 107.51: Operating limitations for small unmanned aircraft.

- Section 107.145: Operations over moving vehicles.

5.20.1   Applying for a CoW. A CoW can be requested by following the instructions and submitting an application at https://www.faa.gov/uas/.

5.20.2   Application Process. The application must contain a complete description of the proposed operation and a justification, including supporting data and documentation (as necessary), that establishes the proposed operation can safely be conducted under the terms of a CoW. A complete listing of Waiver Safety Explanation Guidelines is posted to the FAA's website to assist waiver applicants in preparing their proposals and justifications for applications for waiver. They can be found at https://www.faa.gov/uas/commercial_opera tors/part_107_waivers/waiver_safety_explanation_guidelines/. Although not required by part 107, the FAA encourages waiver applicants to submit their application at least 90 days prior to the start of the proposed operation. The FAA will strive to complete review and adjudication of waivers within 90 days; however, the time required for the FAA to make a determination regarding waiver requests will vary based on the complexity of the request. The amount of data and analysis required as part of the application will be proportional to the specific relief that is requested. For example, a request to waive several sections of part 107 for an operation that takes place in a congested metropolitan area with heavy air traffic will likely require significantly more data and analyses than a request to waive a single section for an operation that takes place in a sparsely-populated area with minimal air traffic. If a CoW is granted, that certificate may include specific special provisions designed to ensure the small UAS operation may be conducted as safely as one conducted under the provisions of part 107. A listing of standard special provisions for part 107 waivers is available on the FAA's website at https://www.faa.gov/uas/.

5.21   **Supplemental Operational Information.** Appendix B, Supplemental Operational Information, contains expanded information regarding operational topics that should be considered prior to operations.

CHAPTER 6. PART 107 SUBPART C, REMOTE PILOT CERTIFICATION

6.1 Applicability. This chapter provides guidance regarding the airman certification requirements and procedures for persons acting as remote pilot in command (PIC) of a small UAS operated in the National Airspace System (NAS). In the aviation context, the FAA typically refers to "licensing" as "certification."

6.2 Remote Pilot Certification. An individual exercising the authority of PIC in compliance with part 107 is considered a "remote PIC." As such, prior to acting as remote PIC, an individual must obtain a Remote Pilot Certificate with a small UAS rating (§ 107.12).

6.3 Eligibility. Pursuant to the requirements of § 107.61, an individual applying for a Remote Pilot Certificate with a small UAS rating must meet the following eligibility requirements, as applicable:

- Be at least 16 years of age.

- Be able to read, speak, write, and understand the English language.

  Note: Please refer to § 107.17 for small UAS operating prohibitions for an individual with known medical conditions.

- Be in a physical and mental condition that would not interfere with the safe operation of a small UAS.

- Pass the initial aeronautical knowledge test at an FAA-approved Knowledge Testing Center (KTC). However, an individual who already holds a pilot certificate issued under 14 CFR part 61, other than a student pilot certificate, and meets the flight review requirements specified in part 61, § 61.56 is only required to complete successfully a part 107 online training, found at https://www.faasafety.gov. For more information concerning aeronautical knowledge tests and training, see paragraphs 6.7 and 6.8.

6.4 Application Process. This paragraph provides guidance on how an individual can apply for a Remote Pilot Certificate (§ 107.63).

6.4.1 Remote Pilot Applicants Without Part 61 Certificates. An individual who does not hold a part 61 pilot certificate or a part 61 certificate holder who does not meet the flight review requirements specified in § 61.56 must use the following process. A part 61 pilot who meets the flight review requirements specified in § 61.56 may elect to use this process.

1. Pass an initial aeronautical knowledge test administered at a KTC (see paragraphs 6.7 and 6.8).

2. Complete and submit the Remote Pilot Certificate and/or Rating Application for a Remote Pilot Certificate (FAA Form 8710-13).

- **Option 1 (Online Form):** This is the fastest and simplest method. The FAA Form 8710-13 application should be completed online using the electronic FAA Integrated Airmen Certificate and Rating Application (IACRA) system (https://iacra.faa.gov/iacra/). An applicant seeking a Remote Pilot Certificate must have already passed an initial Remote Pilot aeronautical knowledge test. Once registered with IACRA, the applicant will log in with their username and password. Click on "Start New Application" and (1) Application Type: "Pilot," (2) Certifications: "Initial Remote Pilot," (3) "Other Path Information," and (4) "Start Application." Continue through the application process and, when prompted, the applicant may select the knowledge test information provided or enter the 17-digit Knowledge Test Exam ID from the knowledge test in IACRA. Knowledge Test Reports upload immediately to the IACRA system. This allows processing the application for certification without any delay after passing the test. The KTC test proctor verifies the identity of the applicant. Once the applicant completes the online application in IACRA, the applicant signs the application electronically and submits it to the Airman Registry for processing. No FAA representative will be required to sign the application if the applicant was able to self-certify.

  Note: When an applicant seeking a Remote Pilot Certificate uses this online option, the application transmits electronically from the applicant to the Airman Registry. The only electronic signature reflected on the IACRA application will be the applicant's. The Registry confirms basic airman information with the Transportation Security Administration (TSA) prior to generating a Temporary Airman Certificate. Once completed, the applicant receives a confirmation email allowing the applicant to log into the IACRA system and print a copy of the temporary certificate.

- **Option 2 (Paper Application):** An applicant seeking a Remote Pilot Certificate could also submit a paper application. If the applicant chooses the paper method, the original Remote Pilot initial aeronautical knowledge test report must be mailed with the application to the following address:

  DOT/FAA
  Airmen Certification Branch (AFB-720)
  P.O. Box 25082
  Oklahoma City, OK 73125

  Note: A Temporary Airman Certificate will not be provided to the remote pilot applicant if the applicant does not hold a part 61 certificate. For this reason, it would be in the applicant's best interest to utilize Option 1 (IACRA system) instead of the paper method, in order to receive a Temporary Airman Certificate once the application has completed the TSA vetting process.

3. Receive permanent Remote Pilot Certificate once all other FAA internal processing is complete.

6.4.2 <u>Applicants with Part 61 Certificates</u>. Instead of the process described above, an individual who holds a part 61 pilot certificate, other than a student pilot certificate, and meets the flight review requirements specified in § 61.56 may elect to apply using the following process:

1. Complete the online Part 107 Small Unmanned Aircraft Systems (small UAS) training located within the FAA Safety Team (FAASTeam) website (https://www.faasafety.gov) and receive a completion certificate.

2. Complete the Remote Pilot Certificate and/or Rating Application for a Remote Pilot Certificate (FAA Form 8710-13).

   - **Option 1 (Online Application):** In almost all cases, the application should be completed online using the electronic FAA IACRA system (https://iacra.faa.gov/iacra/). The applicant must include verification that the applicant completed the online training or passed an initial aeronautical knowledge test. The applicable official document(s) must be uploaded into IACRA either by the applicant or the certifying official.

   - **Option 2 (Paper):** The application may be completed on paper. Using this method, the certificate of completion for the online training must be included with the application. A part 61 pilot, who also meets the requirements of § 61.56, may also take the knowledge test for initial certification. If a part 61 pilot decides to take the knowledge test, the pilot must also include the knowledge test report with their paper application. Please note that the processing time will be increased if a paper application is used.

3. Contact a certifying official such as the local Flight Standards District Office (FSDO), FAA Designated Pilot Examiner (DPE), an Airman Certification Representative (ACR), or a certificated flight instructor (CFI) to make an appointment to validate the applicant's identification. The applicant must present the completed FAA Form 8710-13 along with the online training completion certificate or knowledge test report (as applicable) and proof of meeting the flight review requirements specified in § 61.56. The FAA Form 8710-13 application will be signed by the applicant after the certifying official examines the applicant's photo identification and verifies the applicant's identity. The FAA representative will then sign the application. The identification presented must include a photograph of the applicant, the applicant's signature, and the applicant's actual residential address (if different from the mailing address). This information may be presented in more than one form of identification. Acceptable methods of identification include, but are not limited to U.S. drivers' licenses, government identification cards, passports, and military identification cards (see Appendix <u>D</u>, Remote Pilot Certification and Applicant Identity Verification). If using paper or IACRA method, an appropriate FSDO representative, a DPE, or an ACR will issue the applicant a Temporary Airman Certificate.

   Note: A CFI is not authorized to issue a temporary certificate. The applicant can print their own Temporary Airman Certificate after receiving an email from the FAA notifying the applicant that it is available. The FSDO signs and mails the application to AFB-720 for the issuance of the permanent certificate. Flight instructors may refer to AC 61-141.

6.5 **Security Disqualification.** After the FAA receives the application, the TSA will vet the applicant prior to issuance of a temporary Remote Pilot Certificate. If the vetting is successful, the FAA will issue a permanent Remote Pilot Certificate. If the vetting is not successful, the applicant will be disqualified and a temporary or permanent pilot certificate will not be issued. Individuals who believe they improperly failed a security threat assessment may appeal the decision to the TSA.

6.6 **FAA Tracking Number (FTN) Requirement.** Beginning January 13, 2020, all applicants must establish an FTN within IACRA before taking any FAA airman knowledge test.

- This identification number will be printed on the applicant's Airman Knowledge Test Report (AKTR) in replacement of the Applicant ID number.

- To register for an FTN in IACRA, applicants will need to visit the IACRA website and follow the instructions provided.

- You can access IACRA at https://iacra.faa.gov/iacra/.

- Once you have your FTN, you can register to take your FAA Airman Knowledge Test by going to the following registration and scheduling website operated by PSI Services LLC: https://faa.psiexams.com/FAA/login.

- You can find FTN Frequently Asked Questions (and Answers) at https://www.faa.gov/training_testing/testing/acts/media/ftn_faqs.pdf.

- You can find a video about the registration process for an FTN in IACRA at https://www.youtube.com/watch?v=ETLsH8BruBM&feature=youtu.be.

6.7 **Aeronautical Knowledge Test.** The FAA publishes the Remote Pilot – Small Unmanned Aircraft Systems Airman Certification Standards (ACS) (https://www.faa.gov/training_te sting/testing/acs/) that provides the standards for the Knowledge Test. Materials helpful for preparation are available at https://www.faa.gov/about/office_org/headquarters_office s/avs/offices/afx/afs/afs600/afs630/. Chapter 2, References, lists FAA publications and online resources that will assist in preparing for remote pilot certification.

Note: The following information regarding the knowledge test applies to individuals who do not hold a current part 61 airman certificate.

6.7.1 Knowledge Test. As described in paragraph 6.4, an individual applying for a Remote Pilot Certificate with a small UAS rating must pass an initial aeronautical knowledge test given at an FAA-approved KTC. In order to take an aeronautical knowledge test, an applicant must schedule an appointment with the KTC. On the day of scheduled testing, the applicant must provide proper government-issued photo identification to KTC. The location of the closest KTC can be found at https://faa.psiexams.com/FAA/login. The knowledge test will cover the aeronautical knowledge areas listed below:

1. Applicable regulations relating to small UAS rating privileges, limitations, and flight operation;

2. Airspace classification, operating requirements, and flight restrictions affecting small unmanned aircraft operations;

3. Aviation weather sources and effects of weather on small unmanned aircraft performance;

4. Small unmanned aircraft loading;

5. Emergency procedures;

6. Crew Resource Management (CRM);

7. Radio communication procedures;

8. Determining the performance of the small unmanned aircraft;

9. Physiological effects of drugs and alcohol;

10. Aeronautical decision-making (ADM) and judgment;

11. Airport operations;

12. Maintenance and preflight inspection procedures; and

13. Operation at night.

6.7.1.1 A part 61 certificate holder who meets the flight review requirements specified in § 61.56 may complete training instead of taking the knowledge test (see paragraph 6.7). This training includes the following topics:

1. Applicable regulations relating to small UAS rating privileges, limitations, and flight operation;

2. Effects of weather on small unmanned aircraft performance;

3. Small unmanned aircraft loading;

4. Emergency procedures;

5. CRM;

6. Determining the performance of small unmanned aircraft;

7. Maintenance and preflight inspection procedures; and

8. Operation at night.

6.7.2 Recurrent Training. After an individual receives a Remote Pilot Certificate with a small UAS rating, that individual must retain the level of knowledge required to safely operate a small UAS in the NAS. To continue exercising the privileges of a Remote Pilot Certificate, the certificate holder must successfully complete recurrent training within 24 calendar-months of passing either an initial knowledge test or initial knowledge training. Figure 6-1, Recurrent Training Cycle Examples, illustrates an individual's potential renewal cycles.

Figure 6-1. Recurrent Training Cycle Examples

Individual passes an initial aeronautical knowledge test on September 13, 2020.	Then	Recurrent training must be completed no later than September 30, 2022, which does not exceed 24 calendar-months.
Individual does not pass recurrent training until October 5, 2020.	Then	Individual may not exercise the privileges of the Remote Pilot Certificate between October 1, 2020, and October 5, 2020, when the training is completed. The next recurrent knowledge training must be completed no later than October 31, 2022, which does not exceed 24 calendar-months.
Individual elects to take recurrent training on or prior to September 30, 2020. The recurrent training is completed on July 15, 2020.	Then	The next recurrent training must be completed no later than July 31, 2022, which does not exceed 24 calendar-months.

6.8 Aeronautical Knowledge Training. This paragraph is applicable to individuals who hold a part 61 airman certificate, other than a student pilot certificate, and meet the flight review requirements specified in § 61.56.

6.8.1 Training. As described in paragraph 6.7, an individual who holds a part 61 airman certificate, other than a student pilot certificate, and meets the flight review requirements specified in § 61.56 may complete training instead of the initial knowledge test. The training can be taken online at https://www.faasafety.gov. The FAA offers options for training completion in addition to those available on https://www.faasafety.gov. Other options include completion of special pilot proficiency programs, such as an FAA-provided WINGS course specific to small UAS operations. These programs will offer tools and resources to strengthen decision-making skills and enable the remote pilot to continue to ensure they operate safely within the bounds of part 107.

CHAPTER 7. SMALL UAS MAINTENANCE AND INSPECTION

7.1   Applicability. Section 107.15 requires the remote PIC to perform checks of the small unmanned aircraft prior to each flight to determine whether the small UAS is in a condition for safe operation. This chapter provides guidance on how to inspect and maintain a small UAS. Additionally, Appendix C, Small UAS Maintenance and Inspection Best Practices, contains expanded information and best practices for small UAS maintenance and inspection.

7.2   Maintenance. Small UAS maintenance includes scheduled and unscheduled overhaul, repair, inspection, modification, replacement, and system software upgrades of the small UAS and its components necessary for flight. Whenever possible, the operator should maintain the small UAS and its components in accordance with manufacturer's instructions. The aircraft manufacturer may provide the maintenance program, or, if one is not provided, the applicant may choose to develop one. See paragraph 7.3.5 for suggested benefits of recordkeeping. (See paragraph 8.3.7.4 for Category 4 maintenance requirements. See paragraph 8.3.7.4.1 for Category 4 record retention requirements and owner and operator responsibilities.)

7.2.1   Scheduled Maintenance. The small UAS manufacturer may provide documentation for scheduled maintenance of the entire small unmanned aircraft and associated system equipment. The manufacturer may identify components of the small UAS that should undergo scheduled periodic maintenance or replacement based on time-in-service limits (such as flight hours, cycles, and/or the calendar-days). Operators should adhere to the manufacturer's recommended schedule for such maintenance, in the interest of achieving the longest and safest service life of the small UAS.

7.2.1.1   If the small UAS manufacturer or component manufacturer does not provide scheduled maintenance instructions, the operator should establish a scheduled maintenance protocol. Such protocol could entail documenting any repair, modification, overhaul, or replacement of a system component resulting from normal flight operations, and recording the time-in-service for that component at the time of the maintenance procedure. Over time, the operator should then be able to establish a reliable maintenance schedule for the small UAS and its components.

7.2.2   Unscheduled Maintenance. During the course of a preflight inspection, the remote PIC may discover a small UAS component is in need of servicing (such as lubrication), repair, modification, overhaul, or replacement outside of the scheduled maintenance period as a result of normal flight operations or resulting from a mishap. In addition, the small UAS manufacturer or component manufacturer may require an unscheduled system software update to correct a problem. In the event such a condition is found, flight operations should not occur until the issue is corrected.

7.2.3   Performing Maintenance. In some instances, the small UAS or component manufacturer may require completion of certain maintenance tasks by the manufacturer or by a person or facility (personnel) the manufacturer specifies. Maintenance should occur in accordance with the manufacturer's instructions. However, if the operator declines to use the manufacturer or personnel the manufacturer recommends are unable to perform the required maintenance, the operator should consider the expertise of maintenance personnel familiar with the specific small UAS and its components.

7.2.3.1   If the operator or other maintenance personnel are unable to repair, modify, or overhaul a small UAS or component back to its safe operational specification, the operator should replace the small UAS or component with one that is in a condition for safe operation. All required maintenance should be completed before each flight, and preferably in accordance with the manufacturer's instructions or, in lieu of that, within known industry best practices.

7.3   Preflight Inspection. Pursuant to the requirements of § 107.49, in addition to assessing the intended area of operation and planning the operation as described above in paragraph 5.10, the remote PIC must inspect the small UAS to ensure that it is in a condition for safe operation prior to each flight. This inspection includes examining the small UAS for equipment damage or malfunction(s). This preflight inspection should be conducted in accordance with the small UAS manufacturer's inspection procedures when available (usually found in the manufacturer's owner or maintenance manual) and/or an inspection procedure developed by the small UAS owner or operator.

7.3.1   Creating an Inspection Program. As an option, small UAS owners or operators may wish to create an inspection program for their small UAS. The person creating such an inspection program may find sufficient details to assist in the development of a suitable inspection program tailored to a specific small UAS in a variety of industry programs.

7.3.2   Scalable Preflight Inspection. The preflight check as part of the inspection program should include an appropriate small UAS preflight inspection that is scalable to the small UAS, program, and operation that the remote PIC performs prior to each flight. An appropriate preflight inspection should encompass the entire system in order to determine a continued condition for safe operation prior to flight.

7.3.3   Title 14 CFR Part 43 Appendix D Guidelines. Another option and best practice may include opting to comply with the portions of part 43 appendix D. Although part 43 appendix D is technically a maintenance inspection checklist and not a preflight inspection checklist, it provides a logical and systematic approach to performing an inspection by dividing the aircraft into subgroups. It details inspection of the airframe, then the flight controls, then the batteries, then the engine, etc. Unlike manned aircraft that require significant disassembly, most small UAS inspection items are visible without necessitating the need for disassembly. In the absence of a manufacturer's instructions, an operator may use part 43 appendix D as a guide to develop their own inspection program, but it is not comprehensive, as it does not address unique UAS features like datalinks or support equipment. An operator would need to identify those items not covered and include them in their inspection program.

7.3.4   Preflight Inspection Items. Even if the small UAS manufacturer has a written preflight inspection procedure, the FAA recommends the remote PIC ensure the following inspection items be incorporated into the remote PIC's preflight inspection procedure. Such a practice will ensure the remote PIC accurately determines that the small UAS is in a condition for safe operation. The preflight inspection should include a visual or functional check of the following items.

1. Visual condition inspection of the small UAS components;

2. Airframe structure (including undercarriage), all flight control surfaces, and linkages;

3. Registration markings, for proper display and legibility (part 48, § 48.205);

4. Moveable control surface(s), including airframe attachment point(s);

5. Servo motor(s), including attachment point(s);

6. Propulsion system, including powerplant(s), propeller(s), rotor(s), ducted fan(s), etc.;

7. Check fuel for correct type and quantity;

8. Check that any equipment, such as a camera, is securely attached;

9. Check that control link connectivity is established between the aircraft and the CS;

10. Verify communication with small unmanned aircraft and that the small UAS has acquired GPS location from the minimum number of satellites specified by the manufacturer;

11. Verify all systems (e.g., aircraft and control unit) have an adequate power supply for the intended operation and are functioning properly;

12. Verify correct indications from avionics, including control link transceiver, communication/navigation equipment, and antenna(s);

13. Display panel, if used, is functioning properly;

14. Check ground support equipment, including takeoff and landing systems, for proper operation;

15. Verify adequate communication between CS and small unmanned aircraft exists; check to ensure the small UAS has acquired GPS location from the minimum number of satellites specified by the manufacturer;

16. Check for correct movement of control surfaces using the CS;

17. Check flight termination system, if applicable;

18. Check that the anti-collision light is functioning (if operating during civil twilight and night);

19. Calibrate small UAS compass prior to any flight;

20. Verify controller operation for heading and altitude;

21. Start the small UAS propellers to inspect for any imbalance or irregular operation;

22. At a controlled low altitude, fly within range of any interference and recheck all controls and stability; and

23. Check battery levels for the aircraft and CS.

7.3.5 <u>Benefits of Recordkeeping</u>. Small UAS owners and operators may find recordkeeping to be beneficial. This may be done by documenting any repair, modification, overhaul, or replacement of a system component resulting from normal flight operations, and recording the time-in-service for that component at the time of the maintenance procedure. The operator would then be able to establish a reliable maintenance schedule for the small UAS and its components. The use of hardcopy and/or electronic logbook format for recordkeeping, inclusive of all periodic inspections, maintenance, preventative maintenance, repairs, and alterations performed on the small UAS, is useful in documenting the history of the small UAS. Recordkeeping would include all components of the small UAS, including: small unmanned aircraft, CS, launch and recovery equipment, Command and Control (C2) link equipment, payload, and any other components required to safely operate the small UAS. Recordkeeping of documented maintenance and inspection events reinforces owner/operator responsibility through a systematic means to determine that the small UAS is in a condition for safe flight. Maintenance and inspection recordkeeping provides retrievable evidence of vital safety assessment data defining the condition of safety-critical systems and components supporting the decision to launch. For operators that rapidly accumulate flight operational hours/cycles, recordkeeping of a small UAS may provide an essential safety support. Methodical maintenance and inspection data collection can prove to be very helpful in the tracking of small UAS component service life, as well as systemic component, equipage, and structural failure events.

CHAPTER 8. SMALL UNMANNED AIRCRAFT OVER PEOPLE

8.1   **Applicability.** This chapter provides guidance concerning small unmanned aircraft eligibility requirements and remote pilot responsibilities for small unmanned aircraft operations over people.

8.2   **Category of Operations.** Part 107 establishes four categories of permissible operations over people. Category 1 is limited to a maximum weight of 0.55 pounds, including everything that is on board or otherwise attached to the aircraft at the time of takeoff and throughout the duration of each operation. In addition, the small unmanned aircraft must not contain any exposed rotating parts that would lacerate human skin upon impact with a human being. Category 2 or 3 operations may only be conducted with small unmanned aircraft that fulfill performance-based safety requirements, which limit the risk and severity of injuries based on potential hazards. Category 4 allows small unmanned aircraft issued an airworthiness certificate under 14 CFR part 21 to operate over people in accordance with part 107, so long as the operating limitations specified in the FAA-approved Flight Manual, or as otherwise specified by the Administrator, do not prohibit operations over people.

8.3   **Operations Over People.** Section 107.39 prohibits operations of a small unmanned aircraft over a person who is not under a safe cover, such as a protective structure or a stationary vehicle, unless the operation is conducted in accordance with one of the four categories listed in part 107 subpart D. A remote pilot may operate a small unmanned aircraft over a person who is directly participating in the operation of the small unmanned aircraft. Direct participants include the remote pilot in command (PIC), another person who may be manipulating the controls, a visual observer (VO), or crewmembers necessary for the safety of the small unmanned aircraft operation. A direct participant should be directly involved in the small unmanned aircraft flight operation. The remote pilot assigns and briefs the direct participants in preparation for the operation. The remote pilot may comply with the requirements prohibiting operation over people in several ways. For example:

- Selecting an operational location where there are no people and none are expected to be present for the duration of the operation. If the remote pilot selects a location where people are present, the remote pilot should have a plan of action to ensure human beings remain clear of the operating area. The remote pilot may be able to direct people to remain indoors or remain under safe cover until the small unmanned aircraft flight operation has ended. Safe cover is a structure or stationary vehicle that protects a person from harm if the small unmanned aircraft impacts that structure or vehicle.

- Maintaining a safe distance from people who are not directly participating in the operation of the small unmanned aircraft.

- Ensuring the small unmanned aircraft will not be operated over any moving vehicles.

Note: The remote pilot should consider risk mitigations, and needs to take into account the small unmanned aircraft's course, speed, and trajectory, including the possibility of a failure, to determine whether the small unmanned aircraft would go over or strike a person who is not directly participating in the flight operation.

8.3.1   <u>Minimum Distances from a Person</u>. Part 107 does not impose a specific stand-off distance requirement from people when operating a small unmanned aircraft. The remote pilot may elect to observe a minimum stand-off distance to ensure the safety of the operation. When determining an appropriate stand-off distance, the remote pilot should consider the following factors:

- The small unmanned aircraft's performance, to include course, speed, trajectory, and maneuverability.

- Environmental conditions such as wind, including gusts, precipitation, and visibility.

- Operational area conditions such as the location and movement of people, vessels, or vehicles, as well as terrain features, including structures or any other item that could affect the operational area where the small unmanned aircraft is being maneuvered.

- Probable failures and the ability to perform emergency maneuvers, including emergency landings.

- The remote pilot's familiarity with and ability to maneuver the small unmanned aircraft.

Note: When conducting the small unmanned aircraft operation, the remote pilot should evaluate and make adjustments to this minimum distance from people as conditions change.

8.3.2   <u>Operations Over Open-Air Assemblies of Persons</u>. Remote pilots are prohibited from operating a small unmanned aircraft as a Category 1, 2, or 4 operation in sustained flight over open-air assemblies, unless the operation meets the requirements of § 89.110 or § 89.115(a). This prohibition is subject to waiver.

    8.3.2.1   "Sustained flight" over an open-air assembly of persons in a Category 1, 2, or 4 operation does not include a brief, one-time transiting over a portion of the assembled gathering where the transit is merely incidental to a point-to-point operation unrelated to the assembly.

    8.3.2.2   Category 3 operations are not allowed over an open-air assembly of persons.

8.3.3   <u>Operations Over Moving Vehicles</u>. Part 107 allows small unmanned aircraft operations over people inside moving vehicles with a small unmanned aircraft that meets the eligibility requirements for a Category 1, 2, 3, or 4 operation subject to one of the following conditions:

    8.3.3.1   For Categories 1, 2, and 3 small unmanned aircraft, the operation must be conducted within or over a closed- or restricted-access site. Any person located inside a moving vehicle within the closed- or restricted-access site must be on notice that a small unmanned aircraft may fly over them; or

8.3.3.2   If the operation is not conducted within or over a closed- or restricted-access site, the small unmanned aircraft must not maintain sustained flight over any moving vehicle.

Note: Category 4 small unmanned aircraft may be eligible to operate over moving vehicles as long as the operating limitations specified in the FAA-approved Flight Manual, or as otherwise specified by the Administrator, do not prohibit such operation.

Table 8-1. Operations Over Moving Vehicles – Over or Within a Closed/Restricted Access Site

OPERATIONS OVER MOVING VEHICLES – OVER OR WITHIN CLOSED/RESTRICTED ACCESS SITE				
	Category 1	**Category 2**	**Category 3**	**Category 4**
Directly Participating	Allowed	Allowed	Allowed	Allowed
Not Directly Participating	Must be on Notice	Must be on Notice	Must be on Notice	*Operating Limitations

* Category 4 eligible small unmanned aircraft may conduct operations over human beings and moving vehicles if not prohibited by the operating limitations specified in the FAA-approved Flight Manual or as otherwise prescribed by the Administrator.

Table 8-2. Operations Over Moving Vehicles – Not Over or Within a Closed/Restricted Access Site

OPERATIONS OVER MOVING VEHICLES – NOT OVER OR WITHIN CLOSED/RESTRICTED ACCESS SITE				
	Category 1	**Category 2**	**Category 3**	**Category 4**
Directly Participating	Allowed	Allowed	Allowed	Allowed
Not Directly Participating	Transit Only, No Sustained Flight	Transit Only, No Sustained Flight	Transit Only, No Sustained Flight	*Operating Limitations

* Category 4 eligible small unmanned aircraft may conduct operations over human beings and moving vehicles if not prohibited by the operating limitations specified in the FAA-approved Flight Manual or as otherwise prescribed by the Administrator.

8.3.4   Category 1 Operations. Part 107 establishes a category of operations over people using small unmanned aircraft that weigh 0.55 pounds (250 grams) or less on takeoff and throughout the duration of flight, including everything that is on board or otherwise attached to the aircraft. In addition to weight limits, Category 1 small unmanned aircraft must not contain any exposed rotating parts that would lacerate human skin upon impact. Remote pilots are prohibited from operating as a Category 1 operation in sustained flight over open-air assemblies unless the operation meets the requirements of § 89.110 or § 89.115(a). This prohibition is subject to waiver.

8.3.4.1   The remote pilot is responsible for determining that the small unmanned aircraft does not exceed the weight threshold and must ensure that the small unmanned aircraft does not contain any exposed rotating parts that would lacerate human skin. These requirements are in addition to the already existing pilot requirements of part 107, such as the preflight responsibilities listed in § 107.49 (see paragraph 8.11.1).

8.3.4.2   There are no applicant requirements for Category 1.

8.3.5   Category 2 Operations. To conduct Category 2 operations over people, the small unmanned aircraft must meet the requirements of § 107.120. To confirm such eligibility, the small unmanned aircraft must be listed on an FAA-accepted declaration of compliance (DOC).

8.3.5.1   It is the remote pilot's responsibility to ensure that the small unmanned aircraft is listed on an FAA-accepted DOC as eligible for Category 2 operations and labeled as eligible to conduct Category 2 operations. A remote pilot can accomplish these things by checking the FAA's DOC Portal at https://uasdoc.faa.gov to see if the DOC is valid and by visually inspecting the aircraft to ensure a label identifying the aircraft as Category 2 is affixed to the aircraft. These requirements are in addition to the already existing pilot requirements of part 107, such as the preflight responsibilities listed in § 107.49.

8.3.5.2   Additionally, the small unmanned aircraft must display a label indicating eligibility to conduct Category 2 operations; have current remote pilot operating instructions that apply to the operation of the small unmanned aircraft, which are described below in paragraph 8.12; and be subject to a product support and notification process. (The applicant must submit the DOC containing specific information to affirm that the aircraft meets the safety requirements through an FAA-accepted means of compliance (MOC). See paragraph 8.9 for a detailed description of the DOC and the process for submitting the DOC.)

8.3.5.3   Remote pilots are prohibited from operating as a Category 2 operation in sustained flight over open-air assemblies unless the operation meets the requirements of § 89.110 or § 89.115(a). This prohibition is subject to waiver.

8.3.6   Category 3 Operations. To conduct Category 3 operations over people, a small unmanned aircraft must meet the safety requirements of § 107.130. To confirm such eligibility, the small unmanned aircraft must be listed on an FAA-accepted DOC.

8.3.6.1   It is the remote pilot's responsibility to ensure the small unmanned aircraft is listed on an FAA-accepted DOC and labeled as eligible to conduct Category 3 operations. A remote pilot can accomplish these things by checking online at https://uasdoc.faa.gov to see if the DOC is valid and by visually inspecting the aircraft to ensure a label identifying the aircraft as Category 3 is affixed to the aircraft. These requirements are in addition to the already existing pilot requirements of part 107, such as the preflight responsibilities listed in § 107.49.

8.3.6.2   Additionally, the small unmanned aircraft must display a label identifying eligibility to conduct Category 3 operations; have current remote pilot operating instructions that apply to the operation of the small unmanned aircraft, which are described below in paragraph 8.12; and be subject to a product support and notification process. (The applicant must submit the DOC containing specific information to affirm that the aircraft meets the safety requirements through an FAA-accepted MOC. See paragraph 8.9 for a detailed description of the DOC and the process for submitting the DOC.)

8.3.6.3   **Location Requirements and Restrictions.** Category 3 operations are allowed under the following conditions:

- The operation is conducted over a closed- or restricted-access site and everyone located within the site must be on notice that a small unmanned aircraft may fly over them.

- The operation is not conducted within a closed- or restricted-access site, and the small unmanned aircraft does not sustain flight over any person unless that person is directly participating in the operation or located under a covered structure or inside a stationary vehicle that can provide reasonable protection from a falling small unmanned aircraft.

8.3.6.4   **No Operations Over Open-Air Assemblies of People.** Category 3 operations are not allowed over an open-air assembly of persons. While the FAA does not define open-air assembly by regulation, it employs a case-by-case approach in determining how to apply the term. Open-air assembly has to do with the density of people who are not directly participating in the operation of the small unmanned aircraft and the size of the operational area. An open-air assembly is generally understood as dense gatherings of people in the open, usually associated with concert venues, sporting events, parks, and beaches during certain events. Such assemblies are usually associated with public spaces. The FAA considers that some potential examples of open-air assemblies may include sporting events, concerts, parades, protests, political rallies, community festivals, or parks and beaches during certain events. Some potential examples that are less likely to be considered open-air assemblies include individual persons or families exiting a shopping center, persons participating in casual sports in an open area without spectators, individuals or small groups taking leisure in a park or on a beach, or individuals walking or riding a bike along a bike path. Whether an open-air assembly exists depends on a case-by-case determination based on the facts and circumstances of each case. The remote pilot must assess whether the operational area would be considered an open-air assembly prior to conducting flight operations.

8.3.6.5   **Modifications.** The remote pilot operating instructions may contain details concerning allowable modifications of the small unmanned aircraft. Modifications not allowed by the remote pilot operating instructions may render the small unmanned aircraft ineligible for operations over people. Such modifications would require submission of a new DOC. Additionally, the small unmanned aircraft may need to be relabeled to reflect the category of operations it is eligible to conduct. In the case of the sale or transfer of the small unmanned aircraft, or use of the aircraft by someone other than the applicant, the applicant must provide remote pilot operating instructions that reflect the aircraft's eligible category and acceptable modifications. Therefore, the FAA encourages manufacturers of small unmanned aircraft to keep track of modifications that would require an update to the remote pilot operating instructions.

8.3.6.6   **Closed- or Restricted-Access Sites.** Category 3 operations may take place over or within closed- or restricted-access sites where everyone located within the site must be on notice that a small unmanned aircraft may fly over them, as long as the operational area is not considered an open-air assembly. People who are not directly participating in the operation of the small unmanned aircraft but who are performing functions at the closed- or restricted-access site must be on notice of potential small unmanned aircraft operations, and should be advised of precautions or other recommended actions to take, if necessary. Remote pilots are responsible for ensuring no inadvertent or unauthorized access to the site occur. Adequate assurance could include physical barriers such as barricading and fencing or monitoring personnel to ensure inadvertent or unauthorized access to the site does not occur. Geographical boundaries, such as rivers, canals, cliffs, and heavily wooded areas may serve as effective barriers to restrict access.

8.3.6.7   **No Sustained Flight Over People.** In addition to closed- or restricted-access sites, Category 3 operations may take place outside of a closed- or restricted-access site as long as the small unmanned aircraft does not sustain flight over people not participating in the operation of the small unmanned aircraft. This allows the remote pilot to operate over people, but only for a brief period. The intent of the requirement is momentary exposure, without sustained exposure over one or more persons. Sustained flight includes hovering above any person's head, flying back and forth over a person, or circling above an uninvolved person in such a way that the small unmanned aircraft remains above some part of that person. The remote pilot should adjust the flightpath of the small unmanned aircraft to ensure minimal exposure of the aircraft over people, and may need to discontinue the operation if the flightpaths would require sustained flight over people.

8.3.7 <u>Category 4 Operations.</u> Certification is how the FAA manages risk through safety assurance. It provides the FAA confidence that a proposed product or operation will meet FAA safety expectations to protect the public. Eligible Category 4 small unmanned aircraft must have an airworthiness certificate issued by the FAA under part 21 and must be operated in accordance with the operating limitations specified in the FAA-approved Flight Manual or as otherwise specified by the Administrator. The airworthiness certificate allows small unmanned aircraft operations for compensation and hire.

8.3.7.1 The remote pilot conducting Category 4 operations over people must use an eligible small unmanned aircraft. To operate over people in accordance with § 107.140 and over moving vehicles in accordance with § 107.145(c), the remote pilot must operate the small unmanned aircraft in accordance with all operating limitations that apply to the small unmanned aircraft, as specified by the Administrator. These operating limitations must not prohibit operations over people.

8.3.7.2 Remote pilots are prohibited from operating as a Category 4 operation in sustained flight over open-air assemblies unless the operation meets the requirements of § 89.110 or § 89.115(a). This prohibition is subject to waiver.

8.3.7.3 **Category 4 Maintenance.** In order to preserve the continued airworthiness of the small unmanned aircraft and continue to meet a level of reliability that the FAA finds acceptable for flying over people in accordance with Category 4, the requirements of § 107.140(c) apply. Eligible Category 4 small unmanned aircraft must have maintenance, preventive maintenance, or alterations performed in a manner using the methods, techniques, and practices prescribed in the manufacturer's current maintenance manual or instructions for continued airworthiness (ICA) prepared by its manufacturer, or other methods, techniques, and practices acceptable to the Administrator. Additionally, Category 4 small unmanned aircraft must be inspected in accordance with the manufacturer's instructions or other instructions acceptable to the Administrator and have maintenance, preventive maintenance, or alterations performed using parts of such a quality that the condition of the aircraft will be at least equal to its original or properly altered condition.

8.3.7.3.1 The person performing any maintenance, preventive maintenance, or alterations must use the methods, techniques, and practices prescribed in the manufacturer's current maintenance manual or ICA that are acceptable to the Administrator, or other methods, techniques, and practices acceptable to the Administrator. The person who inspects the small unmanned aircraft must do so in accordance with the manufacturer's instructions or other instructions acceptable to the Administrator. Additionally, the person must have the knowledge, skill, and appropriate equipment to perform the work. The person performing the maintenance, preventive maintenance, or alterations must use parts of such a quality that the condition of the aircraft will be at least equal to its original or properly altered condition.

8.3.7.3.2 The owner or operator must maintain records of maintenance performed on the aircraft as well as records documenting the status of life-limited parts, compliance with Airworthiness Directives (AD), and inspection compliance of the small unmanned aircraft. Owner and operator responsibilities are discussed in paragraph 8.3.7.4.1.

8.3.7.4 **Applicability of Maintenance and Record Retention Requirements.** When a remote pilot operates a small unmanned aircraft in accordance with part 107, having an FAA-issued airworthiness certificate under part 21, the requirements of parts 43 and 91 do not apply. However, a small unmanned aircraft issued an airworthiness certificate may be eligible to operate under part 91, under certain circumstances. Part 107 contains necessary updates to the regulatory text to reflect the applicability of operating rules. Category 4 does not prescribe as many maintenance and record retention requirements as are required by parts 43 and 91, respectively. Therefore, it may be difficult for an owner or operator to switch between operating rules. A small unmanned aircraft operated and maintained in accordance with part 107 may find it difficult to show compliance with the requirements of part 43 and 91. To address this concern, an owner or operator can elect to comply with the relevant parts 43 and 91 requirements, even while operating in accordance with part 107. Under these circumstances, electing to comply with the relevant parts 43 and 91 requirements may help facilitate moving back and forth between operational parts, if desired, because the requirements of parts 43 and 91 are more stringent than those of § 107.140 with regard to maintenance and airworthiness.

8.3.7.4.1 Consistent with other regulatory frameworks, such as parts 91 and 135, the owner is responsible for maintaining the small unmanned aircraft in accordance with the requirements of § 107.140(c). However, if the owner enters into an agreement with another entity to operate the small unmanned aircraft, the operator is responsible for the maintenance and records retention requirements for small unmanned aircraft operated in accordance with Category 4 under part 107. The FAA expects most operators of Category 4 small unmanned aircraft operating under part 107 will also be the owner, or operating under direction of the owner. In this case, the owner is responsible for compliance with the Category 4 small unmanned aircraft maintenance and records retention requirements. To maintain flexibility for those owners of Category 4 small unmanned aircraft who wish to enter into an agreement with another entity for the operation of their small unmanned aircraft without the owner's intervention or control, § 107.140(c) provides the means for the responsibility of maintenance requirements and retention of records to be clearly defined in such an agreement. If so specified in the agreement, the FAA would hold the operator responsible for compliance with the Category 4 small unmanned aircraft maintenance and records retention requirements. An agreement between an owner and an operator may be in the form of a written lease or contract, verbal agreement, or other agreement. If any agreement is found invalid or unenforceable, then the owner has the responsibility to meet these requirements. The provisions of any agreement should address, at a minimum, the requirements of § 107.140(c).

Table 8-3. Operations Over People – Over or Within a Closed/Restricted Access Site

OPERATIONS OVER PEOPLE – OVER OR WITHIN CLOSED/RESTRICTED ACCESS SITE				
	Category 1	**Category 2**	***Category 3**	**Category 4**
Directly Participating	Allowed	Allowed	Allowed	Allowed
Not Directly Participating	*Allowed	**Allowed	Must be on Notice	****Operating Limitations

* Remote pilots are prohibited from operating as a Category 1 operation in sustained flight over open-air assemblies, unless the operation meets the requirements of § 89.110 or § 89.115(a). This prohibition is subject to waiver.

** Remote pilots are prohibited from operating as a Category 2 operation in sustained flight over open-air assemblies, unless the operation meets the requirements of § 89.110 or § 89.115(a). This prohibition is subject to waiver.

*** Category 3 eligible small unmanned aircraft must not operate over open-air assemblies of human beings (§ 107.125(b)).

**** Category 4 eligible small unmanned aircraft may conduct operations over human beings if not prohibited by the operating limitations specified in the FAA-approved Flight Manual or as otherwise specified by the Administrator. Remote pilots are prohibited from operating as a Category 4 operation in sustained flight over open-air assemblies, unless the operation meets the requirements of § 89.110 or § 89.115(a). This prohibition is subject to waiver.

Table 8-4. Operations Over People – Not Over or Within a Closed/Restricted Access Site

OPERATIONS OVER PEOPLE – NOT OVER OR WITHIN CLOSED/RESTRICTED ACCESS SITE				
	Category 1	**Category 2**	***Category 3**	**Category 4**
Directly Participating	Allowed	Allowed	Allowed	Allowed
Not Directly Participating	*Allowed	**Allowed	Transit Only, No Sustained Flight	****Operating Limitations

* Remote pilots are prohibited from operating as a Category 1 operation in sustained flight over open-air assemblies, unless the operation meets the requirements of § 89.110 or § 89.115(a). This prohibition is subject to waiver.

** Remote pilots are prohibited from operating as a Category 2 operation in sustained flight over open-air assemblies, unless the operation meets the requirements of § 89.110 or § 89.115(a). This prohibition is subject to waiver.

*** Category 3 eligible small unmanned aircraft must not operate over open-air assemblies of human beings (§ 107.125(b)).

**** Category 4 eligible small unmanned aircraft may conduct operations over human beings if not prohibited by the operating limitations specified in the FAA-approved Flight Manual or otherwise prescribed by the FAA. Remote pilots are prohibited from operating as a Category 4 operation in sustained flight over open-air assemblies, unless the operation meets the requirements of § 89.110 or § 89.115(a). This prohibition is subject to waiver.

8.4   **Applicant.** An applicant includes any person who produces, designs, or modifies a small unmanned aircraft eligible to operate over people within the United States. An applicant may produce many small unmanned aircraft, sell kits from which to build small unmanned aircraft, or modify a small unmanned aircraft in a way that affects the eligibility of the small unmanned aircraft to conduct a different category of operations over people than it was previously eligible.

8.4.1   An applicant who manufactures and sells a kit that contains all the components and parts from which to build an operable small unmanned aircraft must comply with the requirements of part 107 subpart D, if the aircraft is intended for operations over people. The kit must contain all the components necessary to build an operable small unmanned aircraft, and would not require the owner to purchase any additional materials. Before the kit is sold, the applicant must ensure that the completely assembled small unmanned aircraft, not only its individual component parts, complies with the performance-based safety requirements to determine eligibility using an FAA-accepted MOC and declare compliance. This will ensure that the small unmanned aircraft meets the requirements of part 107 subpart D.

8.4.2   Someone who builds a small unmanned aircraft from separate components and parts not from a kit is an applicant. For example, someone may purchase the parts of a small unmanned aircraft separately, and build the small unmanned aircraft. An applicant is required to submit a DOC in order to conduct Category 2 or 3 operations.

8.4.3   An applicant may be a person who modifies a small unmanned aircraft listed on an existing DOC, resulting in noncompliance with the original declaration. A noncompliance means the small unmanned aircraft has been altered and is no longer in the same configuration as originally declared. If the small unmanned aircraft is changed so that it is no longer eligible for operations over people, a new DOC must be submitted prior to conducting operations over people or moving vehicles within that category. An applicant should specify allowable modifications in the remote pilot operating instructions (please see paragraph 8.12 below for information concerning remote pilot operating instructions). This ensures a remote pilot who may replace parts or otherwise modify the small unmanned aircraft is aware of which modifications would be allowable for the category of operation. An applicant may develop updates for a small unmanned aircraft after the remote pilot takes possession of it, such as a software update or hardware update. To communicate these updates to the remote pilots, the manufacturer should make operating instructions for the new capabilities of the small unmanned aircraft available.

8.4.4   Any person who makes a modification not permissible by the remote pilot operating instructions to a small unmanned aircraft eligible for Category 2 or Category 3 operations over people renders that small unmanned aircraft ineligible. If the person making the modification intends to conduct Category 2 or Category 3 operations over people with the modified small unmanned aircraft, that person is required to take on the responsibilities of an applicant. In this case, the applicant is required to determine the modified small unmanned aircraft meets the performance-based safety requirements for either Category 2 or Category 3, or both, using an FAA-accepted MOC and submit a new DOC. This principle applies to any person who modifies an existing ineligible small unmanned aircraft with the intention of conducting Category 2 or Category 3, or both, operations over people.

8.4.5   Maintenance actions performed on an eligible Category 2 or Category 3 aircraft that do not change the configuration or characteristics of the aircraft would not require a new DOC to be submitted. For example, if replacing propellers is listed as an allowed modification in the remote pilot operating instructions, a new DOC would not be required. However, replacing propellers not covered in the remote pilot operating instructions requires submission of a new DOC to conduct Category 2 or Category 3 operations over people. Remote pilot operating instructions should include a list of allowed modifications for the small unmanned aircraft to remain eligible.

Figure 8-1. Requirement to Submit a DOC for a Modified Small Unmanned Aircraft

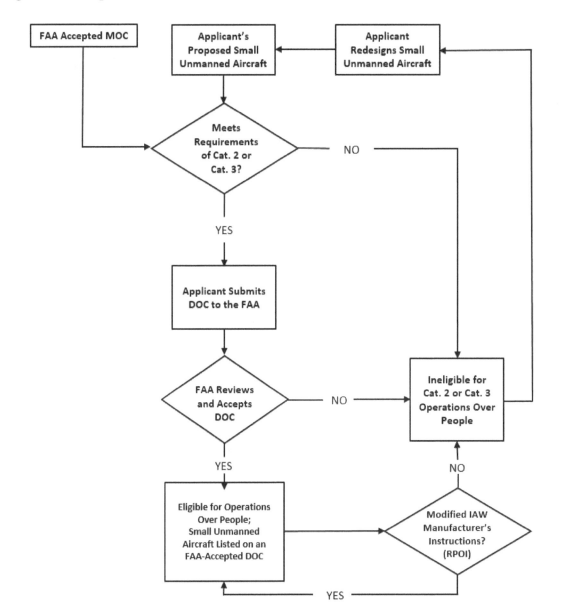

8.5   Means of Compliance—General Information. An MOC is a method to show that a small unmanned aircraft does not exceed the applicable injury severity limit upon impact with a human being, does not contain any exposed rotating parts that would lacerate human skin, and does not contain any safety defects. An MOC must be accepted by the FAA before an applicant can rely on it to declare compliance with the safety requirements for operations over people. Anyone may submit an MOC to the FAA for acceptance if it fulfills Category 2 or Category 3 safety requirements. An individual or a voluntary consensus standards body (e.g., ASTM International or SAE) could develop an acceptable MOC. The MOC must demonstrate through test, analysis, or inspection that the small unmanned aircraft is eligible for operations over people in Category 2, Category 3, or both. The MOC may include consensus standards. Once the FAA accepts an MOC, any person submitting a DOC could use it to establish that a small unmanned aircraft fulfills the requirements of the rule. An applicant requesting FAA acceptance of an MOC must submit certain information to the FAA in a manner the Administrator specifies. When reviewing an MOC, the FAA will utilize a comprehensive set of criteria. The FAA will determine whether the testing, analysis, or inspection described in the MOC demonstrates that a small unmanned aircraft meets the appropriate regulatory requirements. An MOC must address the injury severity limits, the prohibition on exposed rotating parts that would cause lacerations, and verification that there are no safety defects. The FAA will determine whether the proposed MOC aligns with accepted methods used by the medical industry, consumer safety groups, or other peer-reviewed test methods. In addition, the FAA will consider whether the proposed MOC relies on mitigations that require exceptional remote pilot skill or excessive workload to satisfy the requirements.

8.5.1 The FAA must accept an MOC before an applicant can rely on it to demonstrate compliance with the performance-based safety requirements for operations over human beings. An FAA-accepted MOC is subject to an ongoing review by the FAA to ensure the MOC remains valid. If the FAA determines the MOC no longer meets any or all of the requirements to demonstrate compliance with part 107 subpart D, the FAA may rescind acceptance of an MOC. If the FAA elects to rescind an MOC, it will publish a notice of rescission in the Federal Register.

8.5.2 The MOC options an applicant may use are:

1. The FAA-provided MOC, discussed in this AC.

2. An FAA-accepted MOC developed by a voluntary consensus standards body or other entity, or an FAA-accepted MOC developed independent of the FAA. An MOC developed by an individual applicant requires the same level of FAA review as an MOC developed by a voluntary consensus standards body. The FAA generally works with voluntary consensus standards bodies in the development of these standards. As a result, any MOC based on these standards will already have gone through a comprehensive review process during development.

8.6 FAA-Provided MOC. Without prejudice to any other MOC that an applicant may propose and the FAA may accept, the FAA offers one already accepted MOC for both the impact kinetic energy and exposed rotating parts requirements provided at §§ 107.120(a)(1) and (2) (Category 2) and 107.130(a)(1) and (2) (Category 3). The FAA-provided MOC for the injury severity limitations is developed through an applicant's calculation of the small unmanned aircraft's maximum kinetic energy. This MOC does not account for impact dynamics or other factors, but consists of using only the formula the FAA describes to calculate the small unmanned aircraft's maximum kinetic energy. This FAA-accepted MOC provides manufacturers with at least one method to demonstrate their small unmanned aircraft would meet the requirements to operate over people. As a result, the MOC involves confirming (1) the impact of a small unmanned aircraft does not exceed a certain kinetic energy limit, (2) the small unmanned aircraft does not contain any exposed rotating parts, and (3) does not contain any safety defects.

8.6.1   <u>Impact Kinetic Energy</u>. An applicant may use the FAA-provided MOC to satisfy the impact kinetic energy requirements by confirming the impact of the small unmanned aircraft does not exceed the applicable injury severity limits during a typical failure mode at the aircraft's maximum performance capabilities. To test a small unmanned aircraft using this MOC, an applicant would first determine the maximum forward airspeed that the small unmanned aircraft is capable of attaining at full power in level flight. This would be done using a reliable and accurate airspeed measurement method under typical environmental conditions. For example, an applicant could measure the maximum speed using a Global Positioning System (GPS) groundspeed indicator, a radar gun, or tape measure and stop watch. Note that small unmanned aircraft operated under part 107 may not exceed the speed limitations in part 107 unless authorized under a Certificate of Waiver (CoW) or an exemption (§ 107.51(a)).

      8.6.1.1   Next, an applicant would determine the ground impact speed resulting from an unpowered free-fall from the highest altitude the small unmanned aircraft is capable of attaining at full power. Note that aircraft operating under part 107 may not exceed the altitude limitations of that rule unless authorized under a CoW or an exemption (§ 107.51(b)). The ground impact speed could be determined by performing a drop test from the altitude determined in the previous step using a reliable and accurate vertical speed measurement method under typical environmental conditions.

      8.6.1.2   If an applicant determines it is unreasonable to perform a drop test from the highest attainable altitude, then the applicant can perform a drop test from a lower altitude. The lower altitude must be sufficient to determine the small unmanned aircraft free-fall aerodynamic characteristics, such as the coefficient of drag and terminal velocity, to accurately calculate the ground impact speed from a free-fall from the highest attainable altitude. The manufacturer would state in the supporting data the applicant submits pursuant to § 107.155 the environmental conditions under which the applicant determined the maximum speeds. The applicant would also describe any unique test conditions for both the level flight and free-fall scenarios.

      8.6.1.3   The above tests account for speeds a small unmanned aircraft could reach prior to or during a typical failure mode, such as losing power and falling with both a vertical and horizontal speed component. The tests do not take into account small unmanned aircraft failure modes or pilot actions that would cause the small unmanned aircraft to exceed the speeds determined in the previous steps. One example is a powered descent in which the ground impact speed of the small unmanned aircraft exceeds its unpowered free-fall ground impact speed. The FAA assumes these types of failure modes or pilot actions are not typical, and while possible, have a low likelihood of occurring. If an applicant determines these types of failure modes or pilot actions could typically occur and result in speeds greater than those determined in the previous steps, then the applicant should use the higher speeds to determine the maximum impact kinetic energy.

8.6.1.4   Once the applicant determines the maximum speeds associated with a horizontal and vertical impact, the applicant would determine the highest combination of these speeds the aircraft could achieve as a result of a typical failure in order to determine the maximum impact kinetic energy. The applicant should identify and assess typical failures caused by system or equipment loss of function or malfunction as well as those that could be caused by pilot error.

8.6.1.5   In consideration of the maximum speeds and typical failures described above, the applicant should determine the maximum impact kinetic energy using the following equation:

$$KE_{impact} = 0.0155 \times w \times v^2$$

Where KE_{impact} is the maximum impact kinetic energy in ft-lbs, w is the weight of the small unmanned aircraft measured in pounds, and v is the maximum impact speed measured in feet per second (ft/s).

1. For example, a small unmanned aircraft that weighs 1.0 pound and has a maximum impact speed of 26 ft/s has a maximum impact kinetic energy of:

$$KE_{impact} = 0.0155 \times 1.0 \times (26)^2 = 10.5 \text{ ft-lbs}$$

2. Similarly, a small unmanned aircraft that weighs 1.0 pound and has a maximum impact speed of 40 ft/s has an impact kinetic energy of:

$$KE_{impact} = 0.0155 \times 1.0 \times (40)^2 = 24.8 \text{ ft-lbs}$$

8.6.1.6   The two tables below provide examples of maximum impact speeds, rounded to whole numbers, associated with the impact kinetic energy thresholds of the different categories and the weight of the small unmanned aircraft. One table provides speeds in feet per second and the other table provides speeds in miles per hour (mph). Applicants may use these tables when following this MOC based on the maximum performance of the small unmanned aircraft. These tables do not consider any energy absorbing characteristics of a small unmanned aircraft that may reduce the amount of energy that is transferred to a person during a collision.

Table 8-5. Maximum Impact Speeds (ft/sec) for a Given Weight and Impact Kinetic Energy Under FAA-Provided MOC

Weight (lbs)	Maximum speed (ft/sec)	
	Category 2 (11 ft-lbs)	Category 3 (25 ft-lbs)
1.0	26	40
1.5	22	33
2.0	19	28
2.5	17	25
3.0	15	23

Table 8-6. Maximum Impact Speeds (mph) for a Given Weight and Impact Kinetic Energy Under FAA-Provided MOC

Weight (lbs)	Maximum speed (mph)	
	Category 2 (11 ft-lbs)	Category 3 (25 ft-lbs)
1.0	18	27
1.5	15	22
2.0	13	19
2.5	11	17
3.0	10	16

8.6.1.7   If the small unmanned aircraft incorporates airspeed or altitude limiting systems or equipment that, when installed or enabled, restrict its forward airspeed or altitude in order to meet an impact kinetic energy requirement, then those systems or equipment should be installed or enabled when performing the tests described above. If compliance with the impact kinetic energy requirement depends on the proper function of those systems or equipment, then the applicant should provide in the remote pilot operating instructions information on the proper use of those systems or equipment, as well as any restrictions. The FAA anticipates applicants will implement these types of systems or equipment through hardware, software, or a combination of both. If the small unmanned aircraft can be operated with or without these systems or equipment enabled or installed, such as in a variable-mode small unmanned aircraft, then the applicant should provide information in the remote pilot operating instructions to ensure pilots understand any restrictions or limitations associated with the different modes.

8.6.1.8   This MOC does not account for the use or testing of design features such as parachutes, ballistic recovery systems, or other deployable devices that once deployed, reduce impact velocity. Such features can establish that a small unmanned aircraft would impact a person with a reduced amount of kinetic energy. Such design features will require the FAA's review to determine whether they assist in achieving compliance with injury severity limitations. Outside the scope of the FAA-provided MOC, an applicant may choose to demonstrate compliance with the injury severity limitations using deployable devices, as long as the applicant describes how the devices are used to meet the safety requirements in the proposed MOC.

8.6.1.9   The MOC detailed above does not take into account the effect of the small unmanned aircraft's structural configuration or materials of construction during an impact with a person. It assumes that the total kinetic energy of the small unmanned aircraft would be transferred to the person upon impact. In reality, a small unmanned aircraft's structural configuration, materials of construction, or other design features may reduce the amount of the total kinetic energy that is transferred to a person during an impact. The use of energy absorbing materials, or an energy absorbing protective cage, may reduce the transfer of kinetic energy during an impact with a person. Under these circumstances, an applicant may wish to establish the amount of kinetic energy transferred to a person during an impact based on the impact absorbing characteristics of the small unmanned aircraft. If an applicant shows the aircraft does not transfer more than the kinetic energy limit to a person upon impact, the aircraft may be eligible for Category 2 or 3 operations over people. This demonstration would require an MOC that is not provided in this AC.

8.6.1.10   The FAA acknowledges limitations associated with the FAA-provided MOC. The FAA intended with this FAA-provided MOC to provide a test method that applicants could use to show compliance with the injury severity limitations, with the anticipation that industry can and will develop more flexible MOC through a voluntary consensus standards body or otherwise. The FAA expects these industry standards to consider that small unmanned aircraft often have non-rigid structures, which can reduce the kinetic energy transferred to a person upon impact. The FAA encourages the development of such MOC. Please see paragraphs 8.7 and 8.8 below for information concerning other MOC.

8.6.2   Exposed Rotating Parts. One means, but not the only means, of complying with the requirement would be to manufacture the small unmanned aircraft so that it does not contain any exposed rotating parts. For example, if the propellers that provide lift and thrust for the small unmanned aircraft are internal to the unmanned aircraft, such as in a ducted fan configuration, and would not make contact with a person as a result of a typical impact, then the parts would not be exposed. Therefore, the small unmanned aircraft would satisfy this requirement. Testing and analysis may be required to determine that the rotating parts could not become exposed as a result of a typical impact with a person. If the forces on the small unmanned aircraft during an impact with a person are likely to cause structural failures that cause the rotating parts to become exposed, then that design would not satisfy this requirement.

8.7 **Voluntary Consensus Standards Body MOC.** A voluntary consensus standards body incorporates openness, balance, due process, appeals process, and consensus. These characteristics result in a peer review of voluntary consensus standards. Voluntary consensus standards bodies are composed of a wide selection of industry participants, often including the FAA.

8.7.1 The FAA encourages industry stakeholders to develop additional test methods and analyses to provide multiple ways for applicants to comply with the applicable safety requirements. Two potential approaches for industry to consider are provided in the following paragraphs.

8.7.2 A person may develop a standard for small unmanned aircraft having rotating parts that are protected by safety features, such as propeller guards. The standard could require testing by the applicant to support the determination that the protective safety features accomplish their intended function of preventing rotating parts from contacting a person during impact. If the applicant has tested those safety features and demonstrated they would remain intact during impact, this could be one means of demonstrating that exposed rotating parts would not be capable of lacerating human skin upon impact.

8.7.3 If a small unmanned aircraft has rotating parts that are exposed without any protective safety features, it may be shown through testing and analysis that the rotating parts would not lacerate human skin upon impact. By analyzing test data that evaluates the size, shape, rotational speed, material, and orientation of the rotating parts, and the severity of injuries that would be caused by these parts under any impact scenarios, it can be determined that the rotating parts would not lacerate human skin upon impact.

8.7.4 The method of analysis or testing should be commensurate with the applicant's means of compliance. If a small unmanned aircraft has propellers made out of flexible material, an applicant would likely not need to perform sophisticated analysis or testing to demonstrate that the exposed rotating parts would not cause lacerations to human skin upon impact. If an applicant chooses to design a small unmanned aircraft with exposed propellers with sharp leading edges made of a rigid material, such as a carbon fiber composite that are driven by high torque motors, that applicant would likely have to perform a more sophisticated analysis or testing. The objective of the analysis or testing is to demonstrate that the propellers would not cause lacerations upon impact. This testing standard requires the applicant to demonstrate it across a range of typical human encounters and unmanned aircraft operational scenarios. Categories 2 and 3 require the manufacturer to show the unmanned aircraft *would not* cause lacerations (emphasis added). Therefore, the FAA does not expect applications to test for every human encounter, merely the ones that are typical.

8.7.5 The unmanned aircraft may also have a rotor that does not have sufficient momentum to lacerate normal human skin, and may implement technology to stop the exposed rotating part before it would lacerate skin. Another example of how an aircraft could comply with the prohibition on exposed rotating parts that would cause lacerations would be to use materials that are incapable of lacerating human skin. An example of this would be to use or design rotors or propellers with properties that break away or flex upon impact to eliminate lacerations without the use of guards or shrouds. For Categories 2 and 3, any method an applicant chooses to use to comply with the exposed rotating parts requirement must be demonstrated through an FAA-accepted MOC.

8.7.6 Exposed rotating parts may pose a significant laceration hazard if they contact human skin, which is unacceptable for the safety of the public. The FAA distinguishes between a laceration to mean a cut that goes all the way through the skin while an abrasion means a superficial injury to the skin. Additionally, the FAA uses the expression "typical human encounter" to describe normal impacts, such as unmanned aircraft impacting a human being due to a loss of control, small unmanned aircraft failures, or remote pilot error.

8.8 **Means of Compliance.** Any person may propose an MOC to satisfy the safety requirements of § 107.120(a) or § 107.130(a). A person would submit a proposed MOC to the FAA for review and acceptance, showing that its small unmanned aircraft would not exceed the applicable injury severity limit upon impact with a human being, does not contain any exposed rotating parts that would lacerate human skin, and does not contain any safety defects. The FAA must accept an MOC before an applicant can rely on it to declare compliance with the performance-based safety requirements of § 107.120(a) or § 107.130(a), or both.

8.8.1 An applicant requesting FAA acceptance of an MOC should carefully consider the additional time and effort that could be necessary to coordinate an MOC when scheduling its projects. FAA coordination may require the efforts of FAA technical specialists, Chief Scientific Technical Advisors, or other governmental agencies. The use of existing FAA-accepted MOC would be more expeditious because the FAA will already have reviewed such MOC. As with voluntary consensus standards bodies, some developers of an MOC may not be applicants also submitting a DOC to the FAA for acceptance. Guidance for developing and submitting an MOC to the FAA for acceptance is provided below.

8.8.2 An applicant requesting FAA acceptance of an MOC should submit its proposed MOC at https://uasdoc.faa.gov. An acceptable MOC may be used to establish the small unmanned aircraft fulfills the safety requirements set forth in § 107.120(a) or § 107.130(a). The MOC must show, through test, analyses, inspection, or any combination of these options that the small unmanned aircraft meets the safety requirements for the respective category of operation over people. The proposed MOC must include a detailed description of the MOC and an explanation of how applying the MOC fulfills the safety requirements of § 107.120(a) or § 107.130(a), or both. The FAA will evaluate the testing procedure and substantiation documents on a case-by-case basis.

8.8.3 When reviewing an MOC, the FAA will utilize criteria that include, but are not limited to, the following:

8.8.3.1   To evaluate compliance with the appropriate safety requirements, the FAA will determine whether the applicant's methods demonstrate the applicant has properly mitigated the severity of human injury that could occur to an acceptable safety level, as defined in the appropriate aircraft category.

8.8.3.2   The FAA will also determine whether the tests or analyses are performed in accordance with accepted methods used by the medical industry, consumer safety groups, or other peer-reviewed test methods.

8.8.3.3   In addition, the FAA will determine whether the proposed MOC requires unreasonable skill on behalf of the remote pilot or incorporation of mitigations to meet the requirements.

8.8.3.4   The FAA will determine whether the MOC addresses design features such as deployable devices (i.e., parachutes) or other features independent of the small unmanned aircraft to determine whether they assist in fulfilling the safety requirements.

8.8.4   The FAA will indicate acceptance of an MOC by publishing a Notice of Availability in the Federal Register identifying the MOC as accepted and notifying the applicant.

8.8.5   An MOC accepted by the FAA is considered valid whether it comes from a consensus standards body or a person. If a proposed MOC is not accepted by the FAA, the FAA will notify the applicant requesting acceptance of an MOC of any issues with the proposed MOC.

8.9   **Declarations of Compliance.** For a small unmanned aircraft to be eligible to conduct Category 2 or 3 operations over people, the person who designs, produces, or modifies the small unmanned aircraft must declare compliance with the appropriate performance-based safety requirements through use of an FAA-accepted MOC. The FAA will receive such DOCs via an electronic form available on the FAA's website https://uasdoc.faa.gov. Submission of a DOC involves the applicant declaring the following information:

- The applicant has demonstrated that the small unmanned aircraft meets the performance-based safety requirements for the category or categories of operation through an FAA-accepted MOC;

- The applicant maintains a process to notify owners of small unmanned aircraft and the FAA of any unsafe conditions that render those small unmanned aircraft noncompliant with part 107 subpart D;

- The applicant verifies that the small unmanned aircraft does not contain any safety defects; and

- The applicant will allow the FAA access to its facilities and technical documents, records, or reports required or witness any test necessary to determine compliance with the DOC.

8.9.1 <u>Contents of a DOC</u>. An applicant intending to promote a small unmanned aircraft as eligible for operations over people in accordance with Category 2 or Category 3 must submit a DOC to the FAA for acceptance. An applicant submits the DOC through the FAA's website https://uasdoc.faa.gov. A completed DOC will include information the FAA requires for both determining that a small unmanned aircraft complies with the applicable safety requirements and a means of tracking those models of small unmanned aircraft that were declared compliant. In accordance with § 107.160, applicants will declare they have met the requirements of the rule through an FAA-accepted MOC and include the following information:

1. FAA-accepted MOC used.

2. Name of the applicant.

3. Physical address of the applicant.

4. Email address of the applicant (used for correspondence with the FAA).

5. Small unmanned aircraft make and model, and series, if applicable.

6. Serial number or range of serial numbers for the small unmanned aircraft subject to the DOC (open-ended are permitted).

7. Whether the DOC is an initial or an amended DOC, and if amended, the reason for the resubmittal.

8. Declaration that the applicant:

   • Has demonstrated the small unmanned aircraft meets the injury severity limits of Category 2, Category 3, or both, and the prohibition on exposed rotating parts that would cause lacerations;

   • Has verified the small unmanned aircraft does not have any safety defects;

   • Has satisfied the requirement to maintain a product support and notification process; and

   • Will, upon request, allow the Administrator to inspect its facilities and its technical data.

9. Any other information as required by the Administrator.

8.9.2 Additionally, if an applicant resubmits an FAA-accepted DOC, the applicant must include the reason for the amendment. For example, the amendment could include additional serial numbers, document the correction of a safety defect, or correct the misspelling of the applicant's name or an incorrect address. The FAA will maintain a list of FAA-accepted DOCs and make them publicly available on the FAA website. This allows the FAA and the public to determine which makes and models, and series, if applicable, of small unmanned aircraft are eligible to conduct Categories 2 and 3 operations over people.

Note: The Administrative function of the DOC Portal must be used to request a correction to an error or to change certain parts of an applicant's information, such as a name or email address that is currently listed on the FAA-accepted DOC.

8.9.3   After an applicant declares a specific small unmanned aircraft meets the requirements of a particular category, the applicant should ensure the small unmanned aircraft continues to comply with the applicable requirements. By submitting the DOC to the FAA for acceptance, the applicant attests it meets the requirements for part 107 subpart D, including:

8.9.3.1   The applicant declares it has established and maintains a support and notification process to the public applicable to the small unmanned aircraft that are listed on the DOC. The product support and notification process exists to notify small unmanned aircraft owners, the public, and the FAA of safety issues that result in noncompliance with regulatory requirements. Notification to the small unmanned aircraft owners could take the form of a notice on a website or electronic notification to owners. Owners may register their small unmanned aircraft with the manufacturer under a warranty program, or to update the small unmanned aircraft's software. Manufacturer registration may be used to advise the remote pilot that the small unmanned aircraft does not fulfill the safety requirements for eligibility in one or more categories of operations over people. The person who holds the FAA-accepted DOC should exercise due diligence to ensure the communications involving potential noncompliant conditions are communicated to the responsible individual. Manufacturers are encouraged to design and utilize a system to facilitate communication between the applicant and the owners of the small unmanned aircraft. Manufacturers should implement their product support and notification system to communicate corrective actions for safety defects. When the manufacturer can confirm that the safety defects have been corrected for specific serial numbers, a new DOC may be submitted. The manufacturer must verify that those serial numbered aircraft have no safety defects prior to submitting a new DOC.

8.9.3.2   The DOC includes an agreement indicating the person who holds the FAA-accepted DOC will allow the Administrator to inspect its facilities, technical data, and any manufactured small unmanned aircraft when a safety issue warrants that level of FAA involvement. Prior to inspecting the facilities, the FAA will coordinate with the holder of the DOC in advance of the FAA visit to explain the safety concerns. Upon receipt of the FAA notification, the responsible person should be prepared to discuss production and safety procedures, including engineering and quality systems, procedures manuals, and handbooks, when practical. The FAA will expect the responsible person who holds the DOC to be prepared to discuss an evaluation of and proposed solution to the safety concerns. This may include a review of:

- Critical processes (including special processes) and critical suppliers.

- Recent design changes.

- Significant changes in manufacturing personnel, procedures, or inspections.

- Quality issues or escapes.

- Witness any tests necessary to determine compliance with part 107 subpart D.

- Any additional relevant correspondence or data pertaining to issues discovered in the course of new product deliveries or acceptance.

- Service history data and service difficulties.

Note: The FAA expects the responsible person to be prepared with any necessary information regarding the items above and other relevant quality data, procedures, or records available to evaluate the safety concern.

8.9.4 <u>FAA Acceptance of a DOC</u>. If the FAA determines the applicant has demonstrated compliance with the requirements of part 107 subpart D, it will notify the applicant that it has accepted the DOC. All FAA-accepted DOCs will be made available on the FAA's website.

8.9.5 <u>Rescinding a DOC</u>. In determining whether to rescind a DOC, the FAA will consider any safety defect, material, component, or feature on a small unmanned aircraft that increases the likelihood that the small unmanned aircraft could cause a serious injury to a person during an operation over people. If such a condition exists, the FAA will initiate contact with the person who holds the DOC by email notification to discuss resolution of the safety defect. The FAA could rescind a DOC if a small unmanned aircraft is no longer compliant with the applicable safety requirements or the prohibition on exposed rotating parts that would cause lacerations. Additionally, the FAA could rescind a DOC if a small unmanned aircraft contains a safety defect and the applicant is unable or unwilling to correct it or if the FAA finds a DOC is in violation of § 107.5.

8.9.5.1 In a case where a person initially declared a small unmanned aircraft compliant with both Category 2 and Category 3, and the FAA finds it necessary to rescind the DOC for one of the categories, the FAA will take the following actions. First, the FAA will issue a notice to the applicant proposing to rescind the DOC. The notice would set forth the agency's basis for the proposed rescission and provide the applicant 30 calendar-days to submit information to refute the proposed notice of rescission. If the holder of the DOC does not provide information demonstrating that the small unmanned aircraft meets the applicable safety requirements within 30 calendar-days, the FAA will issue a notice rescinding the DOC. In addition to publishing any final rescission of a DOC on the FAA website, the FAA may publish notification of any applicable safety defects in the Federal Register as a Notice of Availability. Such a notice will inform remote pilots that the identified aircraft are no longer eligible to conduct operations over people.

8.9.5.2   If the FAA rescinds a DOC for a small unmanned aircraft because of a safety issue, a small unmanned aircraft can be modified such that the safety issue is resolved. The person may then seek acceptance of the modified small unmanned aircraft by submitting a new DOC. In a scenario in which the FAA previously rescinded a DOC due to a safety issue, the newly submitted DOC will be subject to review by the FAA. The applicant will receive notification from the FAA once the DOC is accepted.

8.9.5.3   If the FAA rescinds a DOC, the FAA will publish the rescission on the FAA website. If the person resolved the safety issue and submitted a new or amended DOC and the FAA determines the person has corrected the safety issue, the FAA will accept the resubmitted DOC.

8.9.6   Emergency Rescission. Prior to rescission of a DOC, the FAA will engage in the safety issue notification process with the person who holds the DOC. However, if the FAA determines an emergency exists and safety of persons requires an immediate rescission of a DOC, the FAA may rescind a DOC without a prior notification as provided in Title 49 of the United States Code (49 U.S.C.) § 46105(c). This emergency rescission would be a final agency action.

8.9.7   Petition for Reconsideration of a Rescission of a DOC. If the FAA rescinds a DOC due to an unresolved safety issue, the person who holds the DOC has the opportunity to petition the FAA for reconsideration. Within 60 days of the date of issuance of a notice of rescission, the person may seek reconsideration by submitting a request to the FAA. The petition for reconsideration must demonstrate that information was not present in the original response and an explanation for why the information was missing, that the FAA made a factual error in its decision to rescind, or that the FAA did not correctly interpret a law, regulation, or precedent. The FAA will consider this petition and issue a final decision either affirming the rescission or withdrawing the rescission. After the FAA issues its final agency decision, the person whose DOC was the subject of the rescission has the option to appeal the action as provided in 49 U.S.C. § 46110. A remote pilot is required to cease operations over people with a small unmanned aircraft listed on a rescinded DOC until final decision has been made on the appeal.

8.10   **Accountability for Holders of DOCs.** Any person who holds an FAA-accepted DOC under part 107 subpart D is accountable for the person's products in several ways. First, applicants must have a way to track their products and to inform the public if their product is deemed unsafe to operate in a particular category for operations over people. Additionally, applicants must allow the FAA access to technical data, as well as facilities, if the FAA determines an operational safety issue warrants that level of involvement. By submitting the DOC, the applicant declares its willingness to abide by these requirements. The FAA may review small unmanned aircraft applicants' procedures, processes, and facilities to determine compliance with this subpart. If the FAA identifies a safety issue that warrants review of an applicant's data, records, or facilities, an applicant will be required to grant access to the information. The FAA expects the holder of an accepted DOC to ensure the following:

- The validity of the MOC to ensure that any injury to a human being upon impact with small unmanned aircraft that is the subject of the DOC does not exceed established safety requirements;

- That the construction of the small unmanned aircraft, related safety analysis, and service history do not reveal the existence of any hazardous conditions or safety defects that could result in noncompliance with the safety requirements; and

- Monitor its manufacturing processes, operational usage, and accident and incident data to ensure the small unmanned aircraft continues to comply with the applicable performance-based safety requirements. This monitoring may also take the form of information received from owners and operators of the small unmanned aircraft.

8.10.1 <u>Safety Defects</u>. The FAA requires holders of an FAA-accepted DOC to comply with this rule by correcting safety defects that would cause a small unmanned aircraft to no longer meet the safety requirements for Categories 2 and 3 operations over people. Any defects identified after the DOC has been accepted must be resolved. If the unresolved safety defect results in the FAA rescinding the DOC, the person correcting the safety issue must submit a new DOC prior to being eligible to resume operations over people. Alternatively, if the holder of the DOC does not correct the safety issue, the owner or operator of the aircraft could correct the safety issue and submit a new DOC, if they are capable and willing to satisfy all eligibility requirements of the DOC. Holders of an FAA-accepted DOC are required to establish and maintain a product support and notification process and provide remote pilot operating instructions for the respective small unmanned aircraft.

8.10.1.1 Safety defects may be identified through a variety of means. The safety defects may be identified through owner complaints, industry safety bulletins, or an individual manufacturer's notification. If the safety defect has been identified by the FAA, we will notify the holder of the FAA-accepted DOC of the defect. The holder will have an opportunity to respond by either correcting the defect or demonstrating the small unmanned aircraft meets the safety requirements. Any rescission of a DOC will be made available on the FAA website. These actions serve to notify remote pilots that the identified aircraft is no longer eligible to conduct operations over people. The rescission of a DOC does not render a small unmanned aircraft inoperable, but rather unsafe and ineligible for operations over people.

8.10.2 <u>Owner and FAA Notification Process</u>. An applicant who seeks FAA acceptance of a DOC will declare on its DOC that it has a process in place to notify owners, the public, and the FAA of any defect of condition that causes the small unmanned aircraft to no longer meet the requirements of the subpart or that it contains any safety defects.

8.10.2.1 If, after submitting and receiving FAA acceptance of a DOC for a particular small unmanned aircraft, the applicant determines that the small unmanned aircraft no longer meets the safety requirements for the category declared, the person must notify the public and the FAA. The notification to the public and owners of the small unmanned aircraft should state that the small unmanned aircraft is not eligible for operations over people until the safety defect has been corrected. The notification to the FAA will describe the nature of the noncompliance and how the applicant will address it. If an applicant chooses to correct the safety defect and submits a new DOC that is reviewed and accepted by the FAA, the applicant should notify the public and owners of that make/model that the small unmanned aircraft is again eligible for operations over people in the respective category or categories.

8.10.2.2 Notification to the public could take several forms, as described in paragraph 8.10.2.1 above. The notice should advise remote pilots that the small unmanned aircraft is no longer eligible to operate over people pursuant to one or more of the specified categories. The FAA expects holders of an FAA-accepted DOC to exercise due diligence to ensure the intended audience receives the communications involving potential unsafe conditions. Applicants should design and utilize a system that facilitates communication with the owners of the small unmanned aircraft. It is important for owners and operators of small unmanned aircraft to be advised that their aircraft may have a safety defect.

8.10.2.3 A holder of an FAA-accepted DOC must notify the FAA of any safety issues it identifies. Although the FAA could use sources other than reports to identify potentially hazardous products, reporting can provide the most timely and effective source of information about small unmanned aircraft. Manufacturers of small unmanned aircraft eligible to conduct operations over people should develop a system for maintaining and reviewing information about their products that might identify when their product has a safety issue that may result in noncompliance for operations over people. This information includes, but is not limited to, consumer complaints, warranty returns, insurance claims or payments, product liability lawsuits, reports of production problems, product testing, or other critical analyses of products. Reporting a safety issue to the FAA would not automatically mean that the FAA would determine that the small unmanned aircraft is no longer eligible to operate over people, or that corrective action is necessary. The FAA would evaluate the report and work with holders of an FAA-accepted DOC to determine if corrective action is appropriate. Holders of an FAA-accepted DOC may notify the FAA of safety issues through the FAA website.

8.10.2.4 As part of the notification to the FAA, the holder of the DOC should include information regarding the nature of the safety issue, and how the manufacturer, the remote pilot, or another party will correct the issue. Once the safety issue is corrected, the applicant will submit a DOC to the FAA for acceptance. Once the DOC has been accepted, the remote pilot may operate that small unmanned aircraft over people in the category or categories for which compliance was declared. If the holder is unable or unwilling to address the safety issue, the FAA may begin the rescission process as described in paragraph 8.9.5. This safety issue may not necessarily render the small unmanned aircraft incapable of operation under part 107; rather, it would only necessarily render the small unmanned aircraft ineligible to conduct Category 2 or 3 operations over people without a waiver, exemption, or corrective action provided by an applicant and accepted by the FAA.

8.10.2.5 If a holder of an FAA-accepted DOC identifies a corrective action to address the safety issue, the holder will provide information to the owners and operators and the FAA regarding how the safety issue may be resolved. If the person implements the corrective action to resolve the safety issue, they must use an FAA-accepted MOC to demonstrate the small unmanned aircraft satisfies the safety requirements to conduct Category 2 or 3 operations over people.

8.10.3 <u>Declaring Compliance for Multiple Small Unmanned Aircraft with the Same Make, Model, and Series (If Applicable)</u>. The FAA encourages manufacturers to establish and maintain a production quality system or design configuration control system to provide for consistent repeatability of the small unmanned aircraft as identified on the DOC. A system may provide increased confidence that each small unmanned aircraft meets the safety requirements for the category of operation for which the applicant has declared compliance. With a system, an applicant can avoid testing every unit that it manufactures.

8.10.3.1 The FAA may request access to facilities for validation of compliance with applicable industry consensus standards and FAA regulations, as necessary. As part of the DOC, the applicant who submits the DOC for FAA acceptance agrees to allow unrestricted access to its facilities upon request by the FAA.

8.10.3.2 It is the responsibility of the remote pilot to ensure a small unmanned aircraft is eligible for operations over people for the category declared before conducting such operations. Before conducting operations over people, the remote pilot must determine whether the aircraft is listed on an FAA-accepted DOC appropriate to the category of operations for the intended flight. The remote pilot may accomplish this by visiting the FAA's website.

8.10.3.3 The FAA will maintain a website listing eligible small unmanned aircraft by make, model, series (if applicable), and category declared that are eligible for operations over people. This FAA website will also indicate those small unmanned aircraft by make, model, series (if applicable), and category that have been found to be in noncompliance with the regulatory requirements through the DOC rescission process. The FAA will publish the final rescission on the FAA website and specify the category of small unmanned aircraft that have been rescinded. If the FAA rescinds a DOC as a result of an unresolved safety issue, the FAA will allow an applicant to petition for reconsideration of the decision or modify the small unmanned aircraft to resolve the safety issue. The applicant could then submit a new DOC that the FAA may accept.

8.10.3.4   The person who holds an FAA-accepted DOC can notify the FAA electronically of a safety issue with the small unmanned aircraft on the FAA's website. When the FAA receives such notification, the FAA will document receipt and may inform the public. The FAA may provide applicant-included information regarding the nature of the safety issue and any other information the applicant provides relating to the safety issue.

8.10.3.5   As part of the notification, the person holding the FAA-accepted DOC should include information regarding the nature of the safety issue and how the safety issue may be corrected. If the person has not determined a corrective action to address the safety issue, the person should advise the public of the nature of the safety issue and a plan for correcting the safety issue. The holder of the FAA-accepted DOC may advise aircraft owners whether operation over people should be continued with their aircraft due to the nature of the safety issue.

8.10.3.6   If the person who holds an FAA-accepted DOC determines a means to correct the safety issue, that person could provide the corrective action information to the owners and operators through their product support and notification system of how the safety issue can be addressed. The FAA will work with the holder of the DOC to determine if the corrective action is acceptable. After the person addresses the safety issue, they must conduct the tests, analysis, or inspections necessary to satisfy the performance-based safety requirements through an FAA-accepted MOC, verify there are no safety defects, and submit a new DOC. When the FAA receives and accepts the new DOC, the FAA-accepted DOC will be provided on the FAA's website.

8.10.4   Recordkeeping Requirements. The FAA requires small unmanned aircraft records related to DOCs be maintained for a minimum of 2 years after the small unmanned aircraft has ceased being manufactured, or the applicant who designs or modifies a small unmanned aircraft must retain the records for 2 years after the applicant submitted the DOC. The detailed description of the MOC and justification showing how the MOC meets the safety requirements for Category 2 or 3, or both, must be retained for as long as the MOC remains accepted. In the event of a safety defect, or if the FAA initiated an enforcement action against an applicant, this information is critical to determine the cause, scope, and severity of the defect or noncompliance. A person submitting a DOC who modifies a small unmanned aircraft must retain all supporting information used to demonstrate the small unmanned aircraft meets the safety requirements of Category 2 or 3.

8.10.4.1   The FAA will access the information described above in several situations. For example, if the FAA becomes aware of a potential safety issue, the FAA will require all substantiating data to determine whether a safety issue exists. The FAA would seek supporting data after any modifications have been made.

Note: For DOCs that are resubmitted, the same recordkeeping requirements will apply.

8.10.5 <u>Holders of an FAA-Accepted DOC No Longer Supporting the Small Unmanned Aircraft Design</u>. A DOC remains valid even in the case of discontinued models. Therefore, the small unmanned aircraft may still remain listed on the FAA website as eligible to operate over people in accordance with the original DOC. However, if an unsafe condition is identified, the FAA may rescind the DOC. Any applicant could submit a new DOC with design changes that rectify the unsafe condition, provided the requirements to submit a DOC in accordance with § 107.160 can be satisfied.

8.11 Product Labeling.

8.11.1 <u>Category 1</u>. The FAA does not require labeling of small unmanned aircraft eligible for Category 1 operations. Marking the retail packaging with the weight of the aircraft, or with a general statement that the aircraft weighs 0.55 pounds or less would be helpful to the consumer. The manufacturer may also provide information to assist the pilot in determining that the small unmanned aircraft does not have any exposed rotating parts that would lacerate human skin upon impact. This type of packaging would also serve to promote the aircraft to consumers wishing to buy a small unmanned aircraft that has minimal operating restrictions. The FAA expects applicants to provide this type of information on the packaging of a small unmanned aircraft for easy identification purposes; however, such packaging is not required. It is the responsibility of the remote pilot to ensure the small unmanned aircraft meets the applicable requirements. Before conducting Category 1 operations, the remote pilot must determine that the small unmanned aircraft weighs 0.55 pounds or less, including everything that is on board or otherwise attached to the aircraft at the time of takeoff and throughout the duration of each operation. Additionally, the remote pilot is responsible for determining the small unmanned aircraft does not contain any exposed rotating parts that would lacerate human skin upon impact.

8.11.2 <u>Category 2 and Category 3</u>. To be eligible for operations over people in accordance with Category 2 or Category 3, the small unmanned aircraft must display a label indicating the category or categories for which the small unmanned aircraft is eligible to conduct operations. Because operating limitations apply to operations under Category 3, the label on the small unmanned aircraft indicating eligibility for operations under Category 3 also serves to inform the remote pilot of the operating limitations that they are required to observe (§§ 107.120(b)(1) and 107.130(b)(1)).

    8.11.2.1 The FAA does not provide a prescriptive labeling requirement that specifies exactly how an applicant must label an aircraft, what size font to use, specific location, etc. Due to the large variety of small unmanned aircraft models that exist, a prescriptive requirement would be inappropriate. Instead, the FAA allows the small unmanned aircraft to be labeled by any means as long as the label is in English, legible, prominent, and permanently affixed to the aircraft before conducting any operations over people. For example, an applicant may use the following labels: "Category 2," "Category 3," "Cat. 2," or "Cat. 3."

The label could be painted, etched, or affixed to the aircraft by any permanent means. The label should be located externally, where it can easily be seen. The FAA does not prescribe a specific location for label placement because of the design variations of small unmanned aircraft. In the case of very small unmanned aircraft, an applicant may need to exercise creativity in determining the location best suited to satisfying the labeling requirement. Locating a label on a non-critical surface will likely prevent wear and removal during normal operations.

8.11.2.2   If a Category 2 or Category 3 label affixed to a small unmanned aircraft is damaged, destroyed, or missing, a remote PIC must label the aircraft in English such that the label is legible, prominent, and will remain on the small unmanned aircraft for the duration of the operation before conducting operations over human beings. The label must correctly identify the category or categories of operation over human beings that the small unmanned aircraft is eligible to conduct.

8.11.2.3   In order to comply with labeling requirements, a remote pilot must ensure the small unmanned aircraft is properly labeled before conducting any operations over people. A clear and legible label enables a remote pilot, an inspector, or a member of the public to identify the types of operations a small unmanned aircraft is eligible to conduct. An aircraft without a clearly legible label would not be eligible to operate over people. If a label degrades and is no longer legible or attached to the aircraft, the remote pilot is responsible for providing a new label before operating over people. The labeling requirement applies regardless of whether a small unmanned aircraft is obtained directly from an applicant or as a subsequent transfer. No pilot may operate the small unmanned aircraft unless the pilot verifies that the label meets the requirements of §§ 107.120(b)(1) and 107.130(b)(1), as applicable. If the small unmanned aircraft was manufactured before the effective date of this rule, or the small unmanned aircraft was otherwise not labeled, the remote pilot is responsible for determining whether the small unmanned aircraft is listed on an FAA-accepted DOC. If the small unmanned aircraft is eligible to operate over people, the remote pilot is responsible for labeling the aircraft in accordance with § 107.135.

8.11.2.4   A label will need to be changed if a small unmanned aircraft is modified for operation in a different or additional category. If the small unmanned aircraft has been modified and is no longer eligible to operate in its previously labeled category, the label must identify the category the small unmanned aircraft is eligible to operate within. The person who performed the modification would have to remove or cover the previous label so only the label with the new eligible category is visible on the aircraft.

8.12 Remote Pilot Operating Instructions. The FAA requires applicants to provide remote pilot operating instructions for a small unmanned aircraft eligible to conduct Category 2 or Category 3 operations upon sale or transfer of the small unmanned aircraft, or use of the small unmanned aircraft by someone other than the applicant. In addition, the applicant should keep the instructions up-to-date to account for any changes it makes to a small unmanned aircraft.

8.12.1   The remote pilot operating instructions must include, at a minimum, the following information:

1. General information, system description, and system limitations, including the category or categories of operations over people that the small unmanned aircraft is eligible to conduct. This information must describe whether the small unmanned aircraft must include a specific component on the aircraft in order to fulfill the performance-based safety requirements of Category 2 or Category 3, or both, for which the small unmanned aircraft applicant has declared compliance. For example, if an applicant has designed the small unmanned aircraft to have a parachute system or other device affixed to the aircraft and that component is provided separately, the remote pilot operating instructions must clearly identify the component that must be attached. Similarly, the remote pilot operating instructions must list components that are eligible or necessary for inclusion on the aircraft.

2. A statement describing allowable modifications to the small unmanned aircraft.

   a. If modifications are allowed, the remote pilot operating instructions must include a complete description of modifications the applicant has determined do not change the eligibility for the category or categories of operations over people for which the small unmanned aircraft has been declared compliant. Such descriptions of modifications include descriptions of the small unmanned aircraft itself as well as any payload that any person may include on the aircraft.

   b. Modifications the applicant describes in the remote pilot operating instructions must be consistent with the basis for the FAA's acceptance of the DOC. Any person, however, who modifies a small unmanned aircraft in a way that will affect the eligibility of the small unmanned aircraft to operate over people under Category 2 or Category 3 is required to submit a new DOC for FAA acceptance before the small unmanned aircraft is eligible to operate over people.

3. A statement regarding whether the small unmanned aircraft has variable modes or configurations.

   a. For a small unmanned aircraft that has such variable modes or configurations, the instructions must describe how a remote pilot can verify what mode or configuration the small unmanned aircraft is in and how to switch between modes or configurations. This information assists the remote pilot in verifying that the small unmanned aircraft is in the correct mode or configuration to conduct a certain category of operations over people.

   b. Similarly, if a remote pilot chooses to operate in a different category of operations over people, or in a mode or configuration that is not permitted for operations over people but is permitted under part 107, that person must be able to discern the necessary information from the remote pilot operating instructions. The remote pilot should not be able to inadvertently change the mode or configuration.

8.12.2 The remote pilot operating instructions must be specific to the particular small unmanned aircraft design. An applicant may update existing instructions to include the required information with the small unmanned aircraft, or the applicant may create a new set of instructions that are specific to operations over people.

8.12.2.1 The FAA does not require the applicant to provide the remote pilot operating instructions in a particular format. An applicant could choose to provide the operating instructions as part of the packaging of a small unmanned aircraft, make them available electronically, or by any other means. Regardless of the manner in which the applicant transmits the instructions to remote pilots, the applicant should ensure the instructions remain up-to-date. Remote PICs should be able to discern clearly the set of operating instructions that are in effect at the time of the intended operation of the small unmanned aircraft over people.

8.12.2.2 Information contained in the remote pilot operating instructions should provide enough detail to enable remote pilots to understand clearly how to configure the small unmanned aircraft to ensure compliance with applicable requirements for operating over people. This information informs the remote pilot and aids in decision making. While the remote pilot operating instructions can aid a remote pilot in operating safely, it is ultimately the responsibility of the remote PIC to determine the safe operational parameters for the operation. A description of each of the elements the FAA requires in remote pilot operating instructions follows.

Figure 8-2. Sample Remote Pilot Operating Instructions.

[Small Unmanned Aircraft Make and Model]

TABLE OF CONTENTS

INTRODUCTION

The [small unmanned aircraft make and model] is a high performance aerial imaging aircraft that the FAA has determined is eligible to operate over people. The system comes fully assembled and includes the aircraft, touch screen ground station and 3-axis gimbal camera capable of 16 megapixel still photos and full HD 60 FPS videos. Operating the [small unmanned aircraft make and model], will enable you to capture remarkable photographs and video footage for a wide variety of applications.

GENERAL INFORMATION

IMPORTANT: This small unmanned aircraft is eligible to conduct operations over people in Category 2 and Category 3 provided the remote pilot complies with the modification instructions. Any modification to the small unmanned aircraft not provided for in the remote pilot operating instructions may affect eligibility for operations over people. Please take the time to read this entire instruction manual for more information on operating safety and according to the Federal Aviation Regulations.

NOTE: Before any person may conduct operations of the [small unmanned aircraft make and model], you should create an account online with [manufacturer's name], at [manufacturer's website]. This will enable you to receive important updates regarding the small unmanned aircraft and its eligibility to operate over people, as well as updates, bulletins, instructional videos and more.

SYSTEM DESCRIPTION

Selection of the FLIGHT MODE

The [small unmanned aircraft make and model] is programmed with three (3) flight modes. The flight mode can be selected via the Flight Mode Control Selection Switch located just above the left-hand control stick. IMPORTANT: Selection of the flight mode determines the category of operations that the [small unmanned aircraft make and model] may conduct over people. The following selection options are available:

Flight Mode G: Any operation not conducted over people.
Flight Mode 2: Any operation conducted in accordance with category 2 operations over people.
Flight Mode 3: Any operation conducted in accordance with category 3 operations over people.

REQUIRED COMPONENTS

Category 2 Required Components

1) The [small unmanned aircraft make and model] Airframe
2) Transmitter and Ground Station
3) USB to Micro USB Cable
4) USB Interface/Programmer
5) 3400mAh 9.1V LiPo Battery
6) 9.1V LiPo Balance Connector Charge Lead
7) AC to DC Adapter/Power Supply
8) 16GB microSD Card w/Adapter
9) CAT 2 Rotor Blades & Guards

Category 3 Required Components

1) The [small unmanned aircraft make and model] Airframe
2) Transmitter and Ground Station
3) USB to Micro USB Cable
4) USB Interface/Programmer
5) 5600mAh 11.1V LiPo Battery
6) 11.1V LiPo Balance Connector Charge Lead
7) AC to DC Adapter/Power Supply
8) 16GB microSD Card w/Adapter
9) CAT 3 Rotor Blades & Guards

OPTIONAL COMPONENTS

The [small unmanned aircraft make and model] is already equipped with a high-definition camera. If you intend to conduct operations over people in accordance with Category 2 or Category 3, you may replace the camera only with a pre-approved camera listed in the remote pilot operating instructions, which may be found on the [manufacturer's] website. Additionally, for operations over people in accordance with Category 2 or Category 3, you may not affix any other payload to the [small unmanned aircraft make and model] unless it is listed in the remote pilot operating instructions, which may be found on the [manufacturer's] website. Any permissible payload you affix to the small unmanned aircraft must be securely attached throughout the duration of all operations that occur in accordance with Category 2 or Category 3. Failure to adhere to these requirements will result in the ineligibility of the [small unmanned aircraft make and model] to operate over people in accordance with Category 2 or Category 3.

8.12.2.3   **Additional Information.** Part 107 currently requires remote pilots to conduct a preflight inspection and ensure that the small unmanned aircraft is in a condition for safe operation. These requirements do not change for operations over people. In fact, a preflight assessment for operations over people should be more complex to account for the additional risk inherent in those operations. For example, the remote PIC should consider:

- The location of the people over whom the small unmanned aircraft would fly.

- The weather and other factors that may play a role in the performance of the small unmanned aircraft.

- The environment and airspace in which the operation is being conducted.

- The remote pilot operating instructions to consider the characteristics of small unmanned aircraft, for example, the expected battery life of the small unmanned aircraft.

8.12.2.4   The FAA anticipates the remote pilot operating instructions, which are required for small unmanned aircraft eligible to operate in Category 2 or 3 of part 107 subpart D, will assist the remote pilot in conducting their preflight check and ensuring that the aircraft is in a condition for safe operation prior to conducting the operation.

8.12.2.5   Although the FAA does not require the remote pilot operating instructions to contain information in addition to the above enumerated items, the FAA encourages small unmanned aircraft manufacturers to provide additional operational information to remote pilots. This information will assist remote pilots in planning operations, decision making throughout the flight, and the overall safe conduct of operations of their small unmanned aircraft by providing valuable operating information about the specific small unmanned aircraft design and capabilities. Manufacturers may wish to develop voluntary standards regarding the information provided in the remote pilot operating instructions. These would provide consistency across small unmanned aircraft remote pilot operating instructions, and the remote pilots would have a clearer understanding of what information would accompany a small unmanned aircraft. Information that a small unmanned aircraft manufacturer may wish to consider providing includes, but is not limited to, the factors in paragraphs 8.12.2.5.1 through 8.12.2.5.3 below.

8.12.2.5.1 Performance, Limitations, and Operating Characteristics:

- Operating temperature limits (high and low limits);

- Weather limitations to include wind, precipitation, and maximum wind gusts;

- Altitude limitations to include maximum operating altitude;

- Range limitations;

- Power source to include endurance, power setting, and consumption levels appropriate to the type of propulsion system (fuel, battery, etc.);

- Airspeed limitations;

- Maximum weights;

- Prohibited maneuvers; and

- Other limitations necessary for safe operations over people.

8.12.2.5.2 Normal, Abnormal, and Emergency Operating Procedures:

- Preflight inspection; and

- Emergency or abnormal procedures.

8.12.2.5.3 Weight and Balance (W&B). Information regarding the W&B of the small unmanned aircraft.

8.13 **Remote Pilot Responsibilities When Conducting Operations Over People.** The remote pilot has additional responsibilities when conducting small unmanned aircraft operations over people. In addition to the other operational requirements in part 107, the pilot is responsible for determining they are operating a small unmanned aircraft in the appropriate category for the type of operation they will conduct. The remote pilot is also responsible for verifying the small unmanned aircraft is properly labeled and listed on an FAA-accepted DOC. The remote pilot should perform all of the recommended preflight actions for all flights described in previous chapters and appendices of this AC.

8.14 **Operations Over People at Night.** The categories and their respective restrictions for operations over people do not change due to conditions of night. The test methods, analyses, or manner of inspection an applicant uses for determining that a small unmanned aircraft meets the performance-based safety requirements are time-of-day neutral. The risk mitigation measures apply equally to day and night operations when operating over people, with specific requirements for both the manufacturer of the small unmanned aircraft and the remote pilot.

8.14.1 If the small unmanned aircraft used in an operation at night is eligible to operate in any category for operations over people listed in part 107 subpart D, then the remote pilot may operate the small unmanned aircraft over human beings at night pursuant to the requirements of §§ 107.29 and 107.39. In declaring any small unmanned aircraft as eligible for operations in Category 2 or 3, manufacturers who produce small unmanned aircraft eligible to operate over people at night will most likely need to consider the mass of an anti-collision light in declaring the small unmanned aircraft fulfills the safety requirements set forth in either § 107.120(a) or § 107.130(a).

APPENDIX A. RISK ASSESSMENT TOOLS

A.1 **Purpose of This Appendix.** The information in this appendix is a presentation of aeronautical decision-making (ADM), Crew Resource Management (CRM), and an example of a viable risk assessment process. This process is used to identify hazards and classify the potential risk that those hazards could present in an operation. It also provides examples of potential criteria for the severity of consequences and likelihood of occurrence that may be used by a small unmanned aircraft remote pilot in command (PIC).

A.2 **Aeronautical Decision-Making (ADM).** The ADM process addresses all aspects of decision making in a solo or crew environment and identifies the steps involved in good decision making. These steps for good decision making are as follows:

A.2.1 Identifying Personal Attitudes Hazardous to Safe Flight. Hazardous attitudes can affect unmanned operations if the remote PIC is not aware of the hazards, leading to such things as: getting behind the aircraft/situation, operating without adequate fuel/battery reserve, loss of positional or situational awareness, operating outside the envelope, and failure to complete all flight planning tasks, preflight inspections, and checklists. Operational pressure is a contributor to becoming subject to these pitfalls.

A.2.2 Learning Behavior Modification Techniques. Continuing to utilize risk assessment procedures for the operation will assist in identifying risk associated with the operation. Conducting an attitude assessment will identify situations where a hazardous attitude may be present.

A.2.3 Learning How to Recognize and Cope with Stress. Stress is ever present in our lives and you may already be familiar with situations that create stress in aviation. However, small UAS operations may create stressors that differ from manned aviation. Such examples may include: working with an inexperienced crewmember, lack of standard crewmember training, interacting with the public and city officials, and understanding new regulatory requirements. Proper planning for the operation can reduce or eliminate stress, allowing you to focus more clearly on the operation.

A.2.4 Developing Risk Assessment Skills. As with any aviation operation, identifying associated hazards is the first step. Analyzing the likelihood and severity of the hazards occurring establishes the probability of risk. In most cases, steps can be taken to mitigate, even eliminate, those risks. Actions such as using visual observers (VO), completing a thorough preflight inspection, planning for weather, familiarity with the airspace and operational area, proper aircraft loading, and performance planning can mitigate identified risks. Figure A-1, Hazard Identification and Risk Assessment Process Chart, is an example of a risk assessment tool. Others are also available for use.

A.2.5 Using All Available Resources with More Than One Crewmember (CRM). A characteristic of CRM is creating an environment where open communication is encouraged and expected, and involves the entire crew to maximize team performance. Many of the same resources that are available to manned aircraft operations are available to unmanned aircraft operations. For example, remote PICs can take advantage of traditional CRM techniques by utilizing additional crewmembers, such as VOs and other ground crew. These crewmembers can provide information about traffic, airspace, weather, equipment, and aircraft loading and performance. If conducting operations over people or moving vehicles, crewmembers can also provide timely information regarding the presence of those not directly participating in the operation. Examples of good CRM include:

A.2.5.1 **Communication Procedures.** One way to accomplish this is for the VO to maintain visual contact with the small unmanned aircraft and maintain awareness of the surrounding airspace and operational area, and then communicate flight status and any hazards to the remote PIC and person manipulating the controls so that appropriate action can be taken. Then, as conditions change, the remote PIC should brief the crew on the changes and any needed adjustments to ensure a safe outcome of the operation.

A.2.5.2 **Communication Methods.** The remote PIC, person manipulating the controls, and VO must work out a method of communication, such as the use of a handheld radio or other effective means that would not create a distraction and allows them to understand each other. The remote PIC should evaluate which method is most appropriate for the operation and should make a determination prior to flight.

A.2.5.3 **Task Management.** Tasks vary depending on the complexity of the operation. Depending upon the area of the operations, additional crewmembers may be needed to operate the small unmanned aircraft safely. The remote PIC should utilize sufficient crewmembers to ensure no one on the team becomes overloaded. Once a member of the team becomes overworked, a greater possibility of an incident/accident exists.

A.2.5.4 **Other Resources.** Take advantage of information from a weather briefing, air traffic control (ATC), the FAA, local pilots, and landowners. Technology can aid in decision making and improve situational awareness. Being able to collect the information from these resources and manage the information is key to situational awareness and could have a positive effect on your decision making.

A.2.6 Evaluating the Effectiveness of ADM Skills. Successful decision making is measured by a pilot's consistent ability to keep themselves, any persons involved in the operation, and the aircraft in good condition regardless of the conditions of any given flight. As with manned operations, complacency and overconfidence can be risks. Several checklists and models exist to assist in the decision-making process. Use the IMSAFE checklist to ensure adequate mental and physical preparation for the flight. Use the DECIDE model to assist in continually evaluating each operation for hazards and analyzing risk. Paragraph A.4.8 and AC 60-22, Aeronautical Decision Making, can provide additional information on these models and others.

A.3 **Hazard Identification.** Hazards related to the small unmanned aircraft and its operating environment must be identified and controlled. The analysis process used to define hazards needs to consider all components of the system, based on the equipment being used and the environment in which it is operated. The key question to ask during analysis of the small unmanned aircraft and its operation is, "what if?" Small unmanned aircraft remote PICs are expected to exercise due diligence in identifying significant and reasonably foreseeable hazards related to their operations. It is recommended that remote pilots document small unmanned aircraft and operating environment hazards in accordance with the hazard identification process described in Figure A-1.

Figure A-1. Hazard Identification and Risk Assessment Process Chart

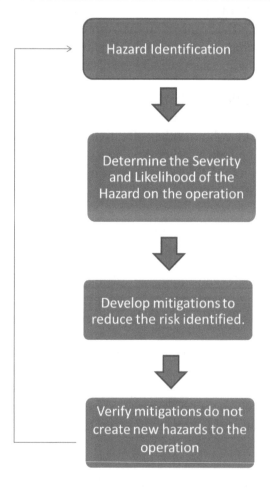

A.4 **Safety Risk Assessment and Mitigation Steps.** Before flight, the following Safety Risk Assessment and Mitigation steps should be taken. Figure A-2 in this paragraph is an example of a risk assessment plan in table format to accomplish this task. This example should not be considered a required format. It is designed simply to show one way to document a risk assessment and mitigation plan.

Figure A-2. Sample Safety Risk Assessment and Mitigation Steps Before Flight

Risk Management – Example of Identified Potential Hazard

Hazard	Cause	Effect	Likelihood (1)	Severity (2)	Risk (3)	Mitigation	Emergency or Contingency Procedures (4)
Describe "what might happen?"	Describe the "why might it happen?"	Describe the effect.	Describe the chances of the hazard occurring.	Describe the consequences if the event does occur.	State the overall risk.	Describe how the risk is minimized.	Describe what will be done if the hazard occurs.
Example: Loss of control link over people	Example: Loss of power supply from control station, small UAS out of range, signal interference from another device (Wi-Fi, Bluetooth, etc.)	Example: Ground impact, injury to people, damage to small unmanned aircraft.	Example: Occasional	Example: Injury to people (possibly including death)	Example: High	Example (partial): The remote PIC must conduct a control link check prior to operations over people. The preflight briefing must include control link loss procedures.	Example: Try to reestablish control link connection with the small unmanned aircraft. If connection cannot be reestablished, start emergency or contingency procedures for loss of control link.

Notes:

(1) **Likelihood:** Likelihood the risk will occur – Improbable, Remote, Occasional, Probable, or Frequent.

(2) **Severity:** Consequence if the hazard occurs – No safety effect, Minor, Major, Hazardous, or Catastrophic.

(3) **Risk:** Combination of Likelihood and Severity – Low, Medium, High, or Avoid (i.e., changes to operation are required for mitigation or the operation should not be conducted). These definitions are used to assign the level of risk prior to consideration of risk mitigation effects.

(4) **Emergency or Contingency Procedures:** This column is your plan of action if the event still occurs.

    (a) In order to identify effectively all potential hazards and their associated risks, you should first begin with a thorough description of the operational environment. This should include (but is not limited to):

        1. Current and forecasted weather conditions.

        2. Condition of the equipment to be used and associated operational limitations.

        3. Remote pilot, observer, and other participants' fatigue and awareness levels.

        4. Terrain and obstacles (such as proximity to power lines, buildings, etc.) in the planned and emergency/contingency flightpath.

        5. Identify the hazard(s) associated with flying over people (hazard column above).

        6. If the operation will occur at night, identify hazards of flying at night, to include those operations whose mission duration includes portions of day, twilight, and night. Such potential hazards include night vision adaptation when unlit towers and buildings are present in the area of operation. Other potential hazards include current and forecast weather conditions and terrain features that may affect the ability for other aircraft operating in the area to see the anti-collision light for at least 3 statute miles (sm).

        7. Identify other hazard(s) present during all small unmanned aircraft flights, such as schedule pressure, health issues, lack of familiarity with equipment, etc. (hazard column above).

    (b) Once you have identified the potential hazards, complete the following steps for each hazard.

    (c) List the cause(s) of each hazard (cause column above).

    (d) List the effect(s) of each hazard (effect column above).

    (e) Perform a qualitative risk assessment by:

        1. Estimating the likelihood of each hazard occurring (probability column (1) above).

        2. Estimating the severity of each hazard, if it occurs (severity column (2) above).

        3. Defining the risk of each hazard as a combination of the probability and severity (risk column (3) above).

(f) Describe the mitigation steps for each hazard (mitigation column above). Develop controls to mitigate all risks to an acceptable level. If such development is not possible, the operator should not operate the small unmanned aircraft until the operator can accomplish this.

(g) Describe any procedures to accomplish, including emergency and contingency procedures, should the hazard occur (emergency or contingency procedure column (4) above).

A.4.1 <u>In-Flight Mitigations</u>. During the flight, the following safety risk assessment and mitigation steps should be taken:

1. Properly use the assessment and inspection checklists, including briefing of appropriate safety risk assessment and mitigation steps.

2. Maintain proper configuration of the small unmanned aircraft for the category of the operation.

3. Constantly re-assess risk.

4. Have and follow procedures for making changes to the flight profile, including crewmember notification.

A.4.2 <u>Post-Flight</u>. After the flight, the following steps should be taken:

1. Perform a thorough debriefing.

2. Capture lessons learned and recommendations.

A.4.3 <u>Contributors to Consider When Performing Risk Assessments</u>. The following list contains examples of factors to consider in assigning a risk rating to a specific identified hazard. This is not a comprehensive list, but an initial list of items to consider:

- Workload.

- Configuration (gross weight, center of gravity (CG), etc.).

- Environment (weather, ATC, particular airport conditions, turbulence, etc.).

- Specific small unmanned aircraft limitations as stated by the manufacturer.

- Consequence of failure in technique, system, or structure.

A.4.4 <u>Formulating Mitigations</u>. Mitigate all risks to an acceptable level. Mitigations are actions to minimize, understand, prepare, or respond to causes of the hazards. They are actions the remote pilot, crewmember(s), or other team member(s) have control over. Mitigations will address reducing either the probability of a cause, the severity of the effect, or both. Mitigations should be detailed and specific in nature. The following items should be considered when formulating mitigations. This is not a comprehensive list, but an initial list of items to consider:

- Set limits on flight conditions (e.g., minimum weather, altitude, minimum/maximum speed, etc.).

- Clearly define and brief criteria that could cause the discontinuation of the flight (e.g., items that affect safety of flight) and who will make and execute decisions.

- Review hazards and specify steps to reduce the associated risk(s).

- Review Weight and Balance (W&B) computations.

A.4.5 <u>Emergency and Contingency Procedures</u>. Describe any emergency and contingency procedures to accomplish if the hazard occurs, despite mitigation steps (emergency or contingency procedure column (4) in Figure <u>A-2</u> above).

A.4.6 <u>Other Risk Assessment Tools for Flight and Operational Risk Management</u>. Other tools can also be used for flight or operational risk assessments and can be developed by the remote PICs themselves. The key consideration is ensuring all potential hazards and risks are identified and appropriate actions are taken to reduce the risk to persons and property not associated with the operations.

A.4.7 <u>Reducing Risk</u>. Risk analyses should concentrate not only on assigning levels of severity and likelihood, but on determining why these particular levels were selected. This is referred to as root cause analysis, and is the first step in developing effective controls to reduce risk to lower levels. In many cases, simple brainstorming sessions among crewmembers is the most effective and affordable method of finding ways to reduce risk. This also has the advantage of involving people who will ultimately be required to implement the controls developed.

A.4.7.1 It is very easy to get quite bogged down in trying to identify all hazards and risks. That is not the purpose of a risk assessment. The focus should be upon those hazards which pose the greatest risks. As stated earlier, by documenting and compiling these processes, a remote PIC can build an arsenal of safety practices that will add to the safety and success of future operations.

A.4.8 <u>Sample Hazard Identification and Risk Assessment</u>.

A.4.8.1 **Example.** I am the remote PIC of a small unmanned aircraft in the proximity of an accident scene shooting aerial footage. Much like pilots in manned aircraft must adhere to preflight action (14 CFR part 91, § 91.103), I must adhere to preflight familiarization, inspection, and aircraft operations (14 CFR part 107, § 107.49). Let's say there is an obvious takeoff and landing site that I intend to use. What if, while I am operating, a manned aircraft (emergency medical services (EMS) helicopter) requires use of the same area and I am not left with a suitable landing site? Furthermore, I am running low on power. If I consider this situation prior to flight, I can use the Basic Hazard Identification and Mitigation Process. Through this process, I might determine that an acceptable level of risk can be achieved by also having an alternate landing site and possibly additional sites at which I can sacrifice the small unmanned aircraft to avoid imposing risks to people on the ground or to manned aircraft operations. It is really a simple process: I must consider the hazards presented during this particular operation, determine the risk severity, and then develop a plan to lessen (or mitigate) the risk to an acceptable level. By documenting and compiling these processes, I can build a collection of safety practices that will add to the safety and success of future operations. The following are some proven methods that can help a new remote PIC along the way:

A.4.8.2 **Hazard Identification.** Using the Personal Minimums (PAVE) Checklist for Risk Management, I will set personal minimums based upon my specific flight experience, health habits, and tolerance for stress, just to name a few. After identifying hazards, I will then input them into the Hazard Identification and Risk Assessment Process Chart (see Figure A-1).

1. Personal: Am I healthy for flight and what are my personal minimums based upon my experience operating this small unmanned aircraft? During this step, I will often use the IMSAFE checklist in order to perform a more in-depth evaluation:

   - **I**llness – Am I suffering from any illness or symptom of an illness which might affect me in flight?

   - **M**edication – Am I currently taking any drugs (prescription or over-the-counter)?

   - **S**tress – Am I experiencing any psychological or emotional factors that might affect my performance?

   - **A**lcohol – Have I consumed alcohol within the last 8 to 24 hours?

   - **F**atigue – Have I received sufficient sleep and rest in the recent past?

   - **E**ating – Am I sufficiently nourished?

2. Aircraft: Have I conducted a preflight check of my small UAS (aircraft, control station (CS), takeoff and landing equipment, anti-collision light for night operations, etc.)? Has it been determined to be in a condition for safe operation? Is the payload properly secured to the aircraft prior to flight?

3. Environment: What is the weather like? Am I comfortable and experienced enough to fly in the forecast weather conditions? Have I considered all of my options and left myself an "out?" Have I determined alternative landing spots in case of an emergency? Will I be flying at night and how may that change the way I operate? What are my associated risks when operating at night? Will I have the ability to see the anti-collision light for at least 3 sm? Will other aircraft that may be operating in the area have the ability to see the anti-collision light for at least 3 sm, considering weather and terrain (certain weather phenomena, such as fog, terrain features, and other phenomena, and obstacles such as hills, mountains, and manmade structures, may affect the ability for me and other aircraft to see the anti-collision light for at least 3 sm)? Is the flash rate sufficient to avoid a collision? Will I be operating over people, and if so, how will I

ensure I do not create any hazards to persons not directly participating in the operation? Can my operational area be considered an open-air assembly of persons? Will I be operating over moving vehicles, and if so, how will I ensure I do not create any hazards to vehicles? Will my operations (landing spots) need to be relocated due to the people?

4. External Pressures: Am I stressed or anxious? Is this a flight that will cause me to be stressed or anxious? Is there pressure to complete the flight operation quickly? Am I dealing with an unhealthy safety culture? Am I being honest with myself and others about my personal operational abilities and limitations?

A.4.9 <u>Controlling Risk</u>. After hazards and risks are fully understood through the preceding steps, risk controls must be designed and implemented. These may be additional or changed procedures, additional or modified equipment, the addition of VOs, or any of a number of other changes.

A.4.10 <u>Residual and Substitute Risk</u>. Residual risk is the risk remaining after mitigation has been completed. Often, this is a multistep process, continuing until risk has been mitigated to an acceptable level necessary to begin or continue operation. After these controls are designed but before the operation begins or continues, an assessment must be made of whether the controls are likely to be effective and/or whether they introduce new hazards to the operation. The latter condition, introduction of new hazards, is referred to as substitute risk, a situation in which the resolution is worse than the original issue. The loop seen in Figure A-1 that returns back to the top of the diagram depicts the use of the preceding hazard identification, risk analysis, and risk assessment processes to determine whether the modified operation is acceptable.

A.4.11 <u>Starting the Operation</u>. Once a remote PIC develops and implements appropriate risk controls, the operation can begin.

APPENDIX B. SUPPLEMENTAL OPERATIONAL INFORMATION

B.1 **Determining Operational Performance.** The manufacturer may provide operational and performance information that contains the operational performance data for the aircraft such as data pertaining to takeoff, climb, range, endurance, descent, and landing. To be able to make practical use of the aircraft's capabilities and limitations, it is essential to understand the significance of the operational data. The use of this data in flying operations is essential for safe and efficient operation. It should be emphasized that manufacturers' information regarding performance data is not standardized. If manufacturer-published performance data is unavailable, it is advisable to seek out performance data that may have already been determined and published by other users of the same small UAS manufacturer model and use that data as a starting point.

B.2 **Small Unmanned Aircraft Loading and Its Effects on Performance.**

B.2.1 Weight and Balance (W&B). Before any flight, the remote PIC should verify the aircraft is correctly loaded by determining the W&B condition of the aircraft. An aircraft's W&B restrictions established by the manufacturer or the builder should be closely followed. Compliance with the manufacturer's W&B limits is critical to flight safety. The remote PIC must consider the consequences of an overweight aircraft, as it may result in an unsafe condition.

    B.2.1.1 Although a maximum gross takeoff weight may be specified, the aircraft may not always safely take off with this load under all conditions. Conditions that affect takeoff and climb performance, such as high elevations, high air temperatures, and high humidity (high density altitudes) may require a reduction in weight before flight is attempted. Other factors to consider prior to takeoff are runway/launch area length, surface, slope, surface wind, and the presence of obstacles. These factors may require a reduction in weight prior to flight.

    B.2.1.2 Weight changes during flight also have a direct effect on aircraft performance. Fuel burn is the most common weight change that takes place during flight. As fuel is used, the aircraft becomes lighter and performance is improved, but this could have a negative effect on balance. In UAS operations, weight change during flight may occur when expendable items are used on board (e.g., a jettisonable load).

B.2.2 Balance, Stability, and Center of Gravity (CG). Adverse balance conditions (i.e., weight distribution) may affect flight characteristics in much the same manner as those mentioned for an excess weight condition. Limits for the location of the CG may be established by the manufacturer. The CG is not a fixed point marked on the aircraft; its location depends on the distribution of aircraft weight. As variable load items are shifted or expended, there may be a resultant shift in CG location. The remote PIC should determine how the CG will shift and the resultant effects on the aircraft. If the CG is not within the allowable limits after loading or does not remain within the allowable limits for safe flight, it will be necessary to relocate or shed some weight before flight is attempted.

B.3 **Sources of Weather Information for Small Unmanned Aircraft Operations.** Remote PICs are encouraged to obtain weather information prior to flight from Flight Service by using the website https://www.1800wxbrief.com. Remote PICs can create a free account in order to use the briefing service. While Flight Service does offer a telephone-based service, it is intended for manned aircraft pilots only.

B.3.1 National Weather Service (NWS). Remote PICs are also encouraged to visit the NWS's Aviation Weather Center (AWC) at https://www.aviationweather.gov. This free, web-based service does not require registration and offers all of the weather products important to a remote PIC, such as Aviation Routine Weather Reports (METAR) and Terminal Aerodrome Forecast (TAF). While reviewing the weather for your intended operation, it is also critical that the remote PIC review any TFRs at the FAA's TFR website, which can be found at https://tfr.faa.gov.

B.4 **Weather and the Effects on Performance.** Weather is an important factor that influences aircraft performance and flying safety. Atmospheric pressure and density, wind, and uneven surface heating are factors that affect small unmanned aircraft performance and must be considered prior to flight.

B.4.1 Wind. Wind speed and direction are important as they affect takeoff, landing, and cruise of flight operations. Geological features, trees, structures, and other anomalies can affect the wind direction and speed close to the ground. In particular, ground topography, trees, and buildings can break up the flow of the wind and create wind gusts that change rapidly in direction and speed. The remote PIC should be vigilant when operating small unmanned aircraft near large buildings or other man-made structures and natural obstructions, such as mountains, bluffs, or canyons. The intensity of the turbulence associated with ground obstructions depends on the size of the obstacle and the primary velocity of the wind. This same condition is even more noticeable when flying in mountainous regions. While the wind flows smoothly up the windward side of the mountain and the upward currents help to carry an aircraft over the peak of the mountain, the wind on the leeward side does not act in a similar manner. As the air flows down the leeward side of the mountain, the air follows the contour of the terrain and is increasingly turbulent. This tends to push an aircraft into the side of a mountain. The stronger the wind, the greater the downward pressure and turbulence become. Due to the effect terrain has on the wind in valleys or canyons, downdrafts can be severe.

B.4.2 Surface Heat. Different surfaces radiate heat in varying amounts. Plowed ground, rocks, sand, and barren land give off a larger amount of heat, whereas water, trees, and other areas of vegetation tend to absorb and retain heat. The resulting uneven heating of the air creates small areas of local circulation called convective currents, which creates bumpy, turbulent air. Convective currents, with their rising and sinking air can adversely affect the controllability of the small unmanned aircraft.

B.5 **Battery Fires.** Lithium-based batteries are highly flammable and capable of ignition. A battery fire could cause an in-flight emergency by causing a LOC of the small unmanned aircraft. Lithium battery fires can be caused when a battery short-circuits, is improperly charged, is heated to extreme temperatures, is damaged as a result of a crash, is mishandled, or is simply defective. The remote PIC should consider following the manufacturer's recommendations, when available, to help ensure safe battery handling and usage.

B.6 **Small UAS Frequency Utilization.** A small UAS typically uses RFs for the communication link between the CS and the small unmanned aircraft.

B.6.1 Frequency Spectrum (RF) Basics. The 2.4 GHz and 5.8 GHz systems are the unlicensed band RFs that most small UAS use for the connection between the CS and the small unmanned aircraft. Note the frequencies are also used for computer wireless networks and the interference can cause problems when operating an unmanned aircraft in an area (e.g., dense housing and office buildings) that has many wireless signals. LOC and flyaways are some of the reported problems with small UAS frequency implications.

  B.6.1.1 To avoid frequency interference, many modern small UAS operate using a 5.8 GHz system to control the small unmanned aircraft and a 2.4 GHz system to transmit video and photos to the ground. Consult the small UAS operating manual and manufacturer's recommended procedures before conducting small UAS operations.

  B.6.1.2 It should be noted that both RF bands (2.4 GHz and 5.8 GHz) are considered line of sight and the command and control link between the CS and the small unmanned aircraft will not work properly when barriers are between the CS and the unmanned aircraft. Part 107 requires the remote PIC or person manipulating the controls to be able to see the unmanned aircraft at all times, which should also help prevent obstructions from interfering with the line of sight frequency spectrum.

B.6.2 Spectrum Authorization. Frequency spectrum used for small unmanned aircraft operations are regulated by the Federal Communications Commission (FCC). Radio transmissions, such as those used to control an unmanned aircraft and to downlink real-time video, must use frequency bands that are approved for use by the operating agency. The FCC authorizes civil operations. Some operating frequencies are unlicensed and can be used freely (e.g., 900 MHz, 2.4 GHz, and 5.8 GHz) without FCC approval. All other frequencies require a user-specific license for all civil users, except Federal agencies, to be obtained from the FCC. For further information, visit https://www.fcc.gov/licensing-databases/licensing.

APPENDIX C. SMALL UAS MAINTENANCE AND INSPECTION BEST PRACTICES

C.1 In the interest of assisting operators with varying background levels of small UAS knowledge and skill, below is a chart offering conditions that, if noticed during a preflight inspection or check, may support a determination that the small unmanned aircraft is not in a condition for safe operation. Further inspection to identify the scope of damage and extent of possible repair needed to remedy the unsafe condition may be necessary prior to flight.

C.2 For Category 4 maintenance requirements for operating in accordance with 14 CFR part 107, see Chapter 8, paragraph 8.3.7.4.

C.3 For Category 4 record retention requirements, see Chapter 8, paragraph 8.3.7.4.1.

Table C-1. Small UAS Condition Chart

Conditions that may result in the small unmanned aircraft not being in a condition for safe operation include, but are not limited to, the following:

Condition	Action
1. **Structural or skin cracking**	Further inspect to determine scope of damage and existence of possible hidden damage that may compromise structural integrity. Assess the need and extent of repairs that may be needed for continued safe flight operations.
2. **Delamination of bonded surfaces**	Further inspect to determine scope of damage and existence of possible hidden damage that may compromise structural integrity. Assess the need and extent of repairs that may be needed for continued safe flight operations.
3. **Liquid or gel leakage**	Further inspect to determine source of the leakage. This condition may pose a risk of fire resulting in extreme heat negatively impacting aircraft structures, aircraft performance characteristics, and flight duration. Assess the need and extent of repairs that may be needed for continued safe flight operations.

Condition	Action
4. **Strong fuel smell**	Further inspect to determine source of the smell. Leakage exiting the aircraft may be present and/or accumulating within a sealed compartment. This condition may pose a risk of fire resulting in extreme heat negatively impacting aircraft structures, aircraft performance characteristics, and flight duration. Assess the need and extent of repairs that may be needed for continued safe flight operations.
5. **Smell of electrical burning or arcing**	Further inspect to determine source of the possible electrical malfunction. An electrical hazard may pose a risk of fire or extreme heat negatively impacting aircraft structures, aircraft performance characteristics, and flight duration. Assess the need and extent of repairs that may be needed for continued safe flight operations.
6. **Visual indications of electrical burning or arcing (black soot tracings, sparking)**	Further inspect to determine source of the possible electrical malfunction. An electrical hazard may pose a risk of fire or extreme heat negatively impacting aircraft structures, aircraft performance characteristics, and flight duration. Assess the need and extent of repairs that may be needed for continued safe flight operations.
7. **Noticeable sound (decibel) change during operation by the propulsion system**	Further inspect entire aircraft with emphasis on the propulsion system components (i.e., motors and propellers) for damage and/or diminished performance. Assess the need and extent of repairs that may be needed for continued safe flight operations.
8. **Control inputs not synchronized or delayed**	Discontinue flight and/or avoid further flight operations until further inspection and testing of the control link between the ground control unit and the aircraft. Ensure accurate control communications are established and reliable prior to further flight to circumvent possible loss of control resulting in the risk of a collision or flyaway. Assess the need and extent of repairs that may be needed for continued safe flight operations.

Condition	Action
9. **Battery casing distorted (bulging)**	Further inspect to determine integrity of the battery as a reliable power source. Distorted battery casings may indicate impending failure resulting in abrupt power loss and/or explosion. An electrical hazard may be present, posing a risk of fire or extreme heat negatively impacting aircraft structures, aircraft performance characteristics, and flight duration. Assess the need and extent of repairs that may be needed for continued safe flight operations.
10. **Diminishing flight time capability (electric powered propulsion systems)**	Further inspect to determine integrity of the battery as a reliable power source. Diminishing battery capacity may indicate impending failure due to exhausted service life, internal, or external damage. An electrical hazard may be present, posing a risk of fire or extreme heat negatively impacting aircraft structures, aircraft performance characteristics, and flight duration. Assess the need and extent of repairs that may be needed for continued safe flight operations.
11. **Loose or missing hardware/fasteners**	Further inspect to determine structural integrity of the aircraft and/or components with loose or missing hardware/fasteners. Loose or missing hardware/fasteners may pose a risk of negatively impacting flight characteristics, structural failure of the aircraft, dropped objects, loss of the aircraft, and risk to persons and property on the ground. For continued safe flight operations, secure loose hardware/fasteners. Replace loose hardware/fasteners that cannot be secured. Replace missing hardware/fasteners.

APPENDIX D. REMOTE PILOT CERTIFICATION AND APPLICANT IDENTITY VERIFICATION

D.1 **Remote Pilot Certification.** Specific knowledge requirements for the Remote Pilot Certificate are located in 14 CFR part 107 subpart C.

D.1.1 A person may apply for a Remote Pilot Certificate with one of the following certifying official: a CFI, a DPE, through an FAA aviation safety inspector (ASI) or aviation safety technician (AST), or with an Airman Certification Representative (ACR) associated with a 14 CFR part 141 pilot school. All Remote Pilot Certificates will be issued by the Civil Aviation Registry Division (AFB-700) on a high quality plastic card stock containing tamper- and counterfeit-resistant features.

D.1.2 Additional information on the eligibility requirements for remote pilots can be found at part 107, § 107.61.

Note: If an applicant has a known medical issue that would require a limitation on the Remote Pilot Certificate, refer that applicant to the responsible Flight Standards office to ensure the application is processed with the correct limitations.

D.2 **Acceptance of a Remote Pilot Application.** Certifying officials may accept an individual's application for an FAA Remote Pilot Certificate by utilizing the FAA's IACRA or the paper FAA Form 8710-13, Remote Pilot Certificate and/or Rating Application.

D.3 **IACRA.** Authorized individuals are encouraged to utilize IACRA for the purpose of accepting a remote pilot application. IACRA is a web-based certification/rating application system that guides the user through the FAA's application process. IACRA may be accessed at https://iacra.faa.gov/iacra/. The website also contains an instruction manual for additional assistance.

D.4 **CFI Registration Process for Accepting an Application for a Remote Pilot Certificate.** In order for a CFI to accept a remote pilot application, the CFI must be registered in IACRA as the role of "Recommending Instructor." Even though the instructor is utilizing the role of a certifying officer, their signature will be reflected in the "Instructor Action" section of FAA Form 8710-13.

D.5 **Establishing Eligibility.** Before processing an application for a Remote Pilot Certificate, the certifying official must ensure the applicant meets the eligibility requirements of § 107.61, meets the flight review requirements specified in 14 CFR part 61, § 61.56, and verifies the applicant's identity. The certifying official should refer to AC 60-28, FAA English Language Standard for an FAA Certificate Issued Under 14 CFR Parts 61, 63, 65, and 107, and the International Civil Aviation Organization (ICAO) website to prepare for the assessment. The AC outlines the required procedures to ensure the applicant meets the FAA Aviation English Language Proficiency (AELP) standards. The ICAO website can be found at http://cfapp.icao.int/rssta/RSSTA.cfm. After conducting an assessment of the applicant's English language proficiency, in accordance with AC 60-28, if it is determined the applicant does not meet the FAA standard, process the application by:

D.5.1 When utilizing IACRA, answer the questions concerning FAA AELP. The system will recognize whether the applicant has met the FAA AELP and process the application as necessary. No additional paperwork will be required to be mailed to the responsible Flight Standards office.

D.5.2 When utilizing a paper FAA Form 8710-13, if the applicant does not meet the eligibility requirements of § 107.61, the certifying official will check the "Application Rejected" box in the appropriate section of the Submitting Official's Report and specify the reason for rejection. The authorized individual will also check the "No" box after the statement "Applicant meets FAA Aviation English Language Proficiency." After verifying the application is complete, forward this application to the responsible Flight Standards office for data entry and processing, even if the applicant does not meet the eligibility requirements. The address and contact information for the responsible Flight Standards office can be found at https://www.faa.gov/about/office_org/field_offices/fsdo/.

Note: If the applicant does not meet the eligibility requirements of § 107.61, *do not* check the "Application Accepted" box. This box should only be checked once it is determined the applicant meets the eligibility requirements. Check the "Application Rejected" box and continue processing the application. The terms "accept" and "reject" are used to notify AFB-700 of whether the applicant meets the requirements for the issuance of a Remote Pilot Certificate.

D.6 **Application Process Utilizing IACRA.** A person who meets the eligibility requirements of a Remote Pilot Certificate may register as an applicant through IACRA, which stores FAA Form 8710-13 electronically until a certifying official accesses the form. FAA Form 8710-13 may be accessed by a certifying official by searching for the person's unique FAA tracking number (FTN) assigned by an FAA internal system after the person has completed the required items on the remote pilot application form. The certifying official will verify that the applicant meets the regulatory eligibility requirements and that the application has been completed properly. Additionally, the certifying official will verify the applicant's identity and input the photograph identification data into IACRA when prompted. Once the authorized individual has completed the application through IACRA, it will be transmitted electronically to AFB-700 for processing.

D.7 **Application Process Utilizing Paper FAA Form 8710-13.** Applicants have the ability to apply for a Remote Pilot Certificate in paper format on the FAA Form 8710-13 to ensure all applicants have the uninterrupted ability to apply for an FAA Remote Pilot Certificate. The same information captured on the paper FAA Form 8710-13 is captured within IACRA. Once it is verified the applicant meets the eligibility requirements of § 107.61, the certifying official will check the "Application Accepted" box in the Submitting Official's Report section. The certifying official will also select the "Yes" box after the statement "Applicant meets FAA Aviation English Language Proficiency." Once the authorized individual has verified that the application was completed in accordance with the form's instructions, the certifying official will send the completed remote pilot application to their responsible Flight Standards office for data entry. The address and contact information for the responsible Flight Standards office can be found at https://www.faa.gov/about/office_org/field_offices/fsdo/. Once the data is captured, the

FSDO will mail the application file to AFB-700 via first-class mail to the following address: DOT/FAA, Airmen Certification Branch, AFB-720, P.O. Box 25082, Oklahoma City, OK 73125. The FAA notes that the submittal of a paper FAA Form 8710-13 may delay the issuance of a Remote Pilot Certificate because of mailing time to AFB-700.

D.8 Documentation of Identification on Paper FAA Form 8710-13. The certifying official accepting an individual's application for a Remote Pilot Certificate should review the person's photo identification presented at the time of application to confirm it is current and valid. The flight instructor should document the type of identification and number submitted (e.g., Virginia driver's license number A12345678 and expiration date xx/xx/xxxx) on the FAA Form 8710-13 "Airman's Identification" section in accordance with the following guidelines.

D.9 Pilot Certificate Applicant Identity Verification.

D.9.1 General Identity Document Review Guidelines:

D.9.1.1 Applicant must present a government-issued photo identification (refer to suggested list below).

D.9.1.2 Confirm that the applicant matches the photo on the identification document.

D.9.1.3 Identity document must be valid. Please note that some States do not provide an expiration date on certain documentation.

D.9.1.4 Name on the identity document must substantially match the name on the application.

D.9.1.4.1 Use best judgment when comparing the identity documents and application data as a person may reasonably identify themselves through the use of multiple variations of their legal, given, and/or nicknames (e.g., Robert Michael Smith Jr; Robert M Smith Jr; Robbie M Smith; Bob/Bobbie Smith).

D.9.1.4.2 Additionally, there may be a suffix on the identity document (such as JR, SR, II, III) that may not be present on the application. Ensure the applicant's name on the application matches their identification.

D.9.1.5 If date of birth is present on the document provided, it must match the date of birth on the application.

D.9.1.6 If address is present on the document provided, compare to the address on the application. If the address is different, please request the applicant to provide a current address.

D.9.1.7 If gender is present on the document provided, it must match the gender on the application.

D.9.1.8 If an identity document appears to be fraudulent or shows signs of tampering, or if any of the identifying information on the identity document does not satisfactorily match the information on the application as explained in this guidance, do not challenge the individual; complete the application process, copy presented documents and record the individual's name, address, and contact information to include phone numbers, emails, etc. Provide this information to supervisory, security, investigative, or law enforcement personnel as soon as possible.

D.9.2 <u>List of Acceptable Documents or Combination of Documents:</u>

1. Unexpired U.S. passport (book or card).

2. Unexpired Enhanced Tribal Card (ETC).

3. Unexpired Free and Secure Trade (FAST) Card.

4. Unexpired Global Entry Card.

5. Unexpired U.S. Enhanced Driver's License (EDL) or Unexpired Enhanced Identification Card (EID).

6. Permanent Resident Card (Form I-551), commonly referred to as a "Green Card."

7. Unexpired foreign passport.

8. Unexpired Reentry Permit (Form I-327).

9. Unexpired driver's license issued by a State or outlying possession of the United States.

10. Unexpired temporary driver's license plus expired driver's license.

11. Unexpired photo ID card issued by a State or outlying possession of the United States. This must include a State or State agency seal or logo (such as a State university ID). Permits are not considered valid identity documents (such as gun permits).

12. Unexpired photo ID card issued by a regional, county, or city/municipal governmental authority, to include but not limited to law enforcement, governmental, education, transportation, or utility authority.

13. Unexpired U.S. military ID card.

14. Unexpired U.S. retired military ID card.

15. Unexpired U.S. military dependent's card.

16. Native American tribal document with photo.

17. Unexpired Department of Homeland Security (DHS)/Transportation Security Administration (TSA) Transportation Worker Identification Credential (TWIC).

18. Unexpired Merchant Mariner Credential (MMC).

19. U.S. Birth Certificate and an unexpired government-issued ID.

20. U.S. Naturalization Certificate with a raised seal, or Certificate of Naturalization issued by U.S. Citizenship and Immigration Services (USCIS) or the Immigration and Naturalization Service (INS) (Form N-550 or N-570) with a government-issued ID.

21. Certificate of Birth Abroad with raised seal, Department of State Form FS-545, or DS-1350 with government-issued ID.

22. Certificate of U.S. Citizenship with raised seal, or Certificate of Citizenship issued by USCIS or INS, or Certificate of Repatriation issued by USCIS or INS, together with a government-issued ID.

23. A Federal agency's written certification of its employee's U.S. citizenship, if the training is being conducted on behalf of that agency.

APPENDIX E. SAMPLE PREFLIGHT ASSESSMENT AND INSPECTION CHECKLIST

E.1   Sample Preflight Assessment and Inspection Checklist. Remote pilots may choose to use this checklist or develop their own for the operation of their specific small UAS.

Preflight Assessment

1. Operating Environment:

    a. Local Weather Conditions;

    b. Local Airspace, ATC coordination/communication requirements, and any flight restrictions;

    c. Identify the location of persons and property on the surface; and

    d. Other ground hazards.

2. Crew Briefings:

    a. Operating Conditions,

    b. Purpose of Flight,

    c. Potential Hazards,

    d. Emergency Procedures,

    e. Contingency Procedures,

    f. Crewmember Roles and Responsibilities, and

    g. Human Factors (I.M.S.A.F.E).

3. Ensure all required documentation is available for inspection.

4. Verify all the manufacturer-required components that make up the small UAS are present and operating as designed.

5. Review Remote Pilot Operating Instructions (if applicable).

6. Complete Certificate of Waiver (CoW) review (if applicable). Review risk assessment and required mitigations.

7. Verify that the control station (CS) location, take-off and landing site(s), including emergency or alternate landing areas are suitable.

8. For operations that will not occur over human beings:

    a. Consider whether lateral and vertical off-sets from human beings will be necessary to maintain safety of the operation.

    b. Review and adjust the flightpath to ensure it accounts for any movement of human beings.

9. For operations that will occur over human beings:

   a. Verify the small unmanned aircraft is eligible to conduct the intended category of operations over human beings.

   b. Verify the small unmanned aircraft is clearly labeled for the intended category of operations over human beings.

   c. If the small unmanned aircraft has undergone any modification, verify the manufacturer allowed such modifications as described in the remote pilot operating instructions.

   d. Verify the small unmanned aircraft is properly configured and mode selected for the category of operations over human beings.

   e. Consider whether the operational area can be considered an open-air assembly of persons.

   f. For Category 3 operations:

      i. Ensure the small unmanned aircraft flightpath of the operation does not go over an open-air assembly of people.

      ii. Not within or over a closed- or restricted-access site: May only operate the small unmanned aircraft above any human being if the operation does not maintain sustained flight over any person, unless the person is directly participating in the operation or located under a covered structure or inside a stationary vehicle.

      iii. Within or over a closed- or restricted-access site: May only operate the small unmanned aircraft above any human being if the operation is within or over a closed- or restricted-access site and any human being located within the closed- or restricted-access site is on notice that a small unmanned aircraft may fly over them.

10. Evaluate and use mitigations to prevent the remote pilot from becoming distracted or losing VLOS during flight operations.

11. Review small unmanned aircraft performance capabilities, considering density altitude and wind, to ensure positive control of the small unmanned aircraft can be maintained and at a safe distance over people, if applicable. The review should also include maintaining a clear flightpath while operating the small unmanned aircraft.

12. Visual condition inspection of the small UAS components.

13. Airframe structure (including undercarriage), all flight control surfaces, and linkages.

14. Registration markings, for proper display and legibility.

15. Moveable control surface(s), including airframe attachment point(s).

16. Servo motor(s), including attachment point(s).

17. Propulsion system, including powerplant(s), propeller(s), rotor(s), ducted fan(s), etc.

18. Check fuel for correct type and quantity.

19. Check that any equipment, such as a camera, is securely attached.

20. Verify all systems (e.g., aircraft and control unit) have an adequate power supply for the intended operation and are functioning properly.

21. Verify adequate communication between CS and small unmanned aircraft exists; check to ensure the small UAS has acquired GPS location from the minimum number of satellites specified by the manufacturer.

22. Verify correct indications from avionics, including control link transceiver, communication/navigation equipment, and antenna(s).

23. Check the display panel, if used, is functioning properly.

24. Check ground support equipment, including takeoff and landing systems, for proper operation.

25. Check for correct movement of control surfaces using the CS.

26. Check flight termination system, if installed (if applicable).

27. Check the anti-collision light is functioning and can be seen for at least 3 sm (for operations that will occur at civil twilight or night).

28. Calibrate small UAS compass, if required, prior to any flight.

29. Verify controller operation for heading and altitude.

30. Start the small unmanned aircraft propellers to inspect for any imbalance or irregular operation.

31. At a controlled low altitude, fly within range of any interference and recheck all controls and stability.

Post-Flight

1. Evaluate small UAS to determine whether repairs are required prior to subsequent flights.

2. Conduct a review of the flight to include any crewmember(s) utilized. This review should consist of items, such as:

   - Remote pilot and crewmember performance of assigned duties;

   - Equipment malfunctions and anomalies;

   - Whether the planned risk mitigation measures were effective or require revision;

   - Unanticipated risks and hazards encountered during flight operations, and mitigations used; and

   - Crewmember concerns and feedback to improve the safety of future flight operations.

Made in United States
Troutdale, OR
10/08/2024

23547175R00060